高校英语选修课系列教材

ACADEMIC ENGLISH READING COURSE

学术英语阅读教程

主　编　陈　勇　官芬芬
副主编　王宗英　李泽明
编　者　胡步芬　张志宾

清华大学出版社
北京

内 容 简 介

本教材以英语学术思维训练为中心，以提高学生学术英语阅读技能为目标，遵循以读促写的原则，重点培养学生做文献阅读笔记、提取关键信息、把握学术语言、识别学术语篇组织结构等阅读技能，从宏观和微观两个层面帮助学生掌握国际通用的学术规范，学会用科学的思维阐述科学问题，讲好科学故事。全书共 8 个单元，每个单元包括阅读文章和学术思维练习题两个板块，Introduction to Academic English Reading Strategies and Skills 部分则对学术英语阅读策略和技能进行了集中阐释。本教材还有配套的 PPT 课件以及参考答案，读者可登录 ftp://ftp.tup.tsinghua.edu.cn 下载使用。

本教材适用于我国高等院校学术英语课程，也可供对学术英语阅读感兴趣的读者使用。

版权所有，侵权必究。举报：010-62782989，beiqinquan@tup.tsinghua.edu.cn。

图书在版编目（CIP）数据

学术英语阅读教程/陈勇，官芬芬主编．—北京：清华大学出版社，2022.8
高校英语选修课系列教材
ISBN 978-7-302-61314-5

Ⅰ.①学… Ⅱ.①陈…②官… Ⅲ.①英语—阅读教学—高等学校—教材 Ⅳ.①H319.4

中国版本图书馆 CIP 数据核字（2022）第 122345 号

责任编辑：刘　艳
封面设计：子　一
责任校对：王凤芝
责任印制：丛怀宇

出版发行：清华大学出版社
网　　址：http://www.tup.com.cn，http://www.wqbook.com
地　　址：北京清华大学学研大厦 A 座　　邮　编：100084
社 总 机：010-83470000　　邮　购：010-62786544
投稿与读者服务：010-62776969，c-service@tup.tsinghua.edu.cn
质量反馈：010-62772015，zhiliang@tup.tsinghua.edu.cn

印 装 者：北京同文印刷有限责任公司
经　　销：全国新华书店
开　　本：185mm×260mm　　印　张：13.5　　字　数：272 千字
版　　次：2022 年 9 月第 1 版　　　　　　　　印　次：2022 年 9 月第 1 次印刷
定　　价：58.00 元

产品编号：098068-01

前 言
Foreword

  2019年中共中央、国务院印发的《中国教育现代化2035》指出，要提升一流人才培养与创新能力，建设一流专业与一流学科。"双一流"建设的关键，就是要培养一流人才，而培养一流人才的关键则在于提升大学生的学习研究能力和国际交流能力。培养懂外语的国际化复合型新工科、新农科、新医科、新文科拔尖和创新人才已成为新时代国家对大学英语教学的最大需求。要实现这一目标，就要求大学生具备用英语阅读国际前沿文献信息，用英语发表研究成果，从容参与国际交流的能力，并养成良好的科学素养和学术思维。在国家人才需求已经发生重大变化的今天，大学英语教学的定位也必须发生根本性的变化，即从以提高语言基础为主的通用英语向以满足大学生科研与学术交流需求的学术英语转变。然而，目前学术英语并没有完全覆盖大学英语课程，相应的教材也跟不上时代发展进步的需要。

  当前，大学生在完成高中英语和大学英语基础课程之后，已经掌握了较为扎实的语言知识和技能，但要应用于英语学术文献的阅读还有相当的困难，原因就在于学术英语与普通英语存在较大的差异。为了填补普通英语与学术英语之间的空白，很多高校开设了学术英语课程，试图在两者之间架设一座桥梁，让学生顺利进入学术英语的学习。然而，由于学术英语不是主干课程，且大多数院校缺乏专门的学术英语教师，学术英语课程建设，尤其是教材建设，面临着很大的挑战。笔者在长期的学术英语教学实践中发现，在为数不多的学术英语教材中，科学思想和学术思维没有很好地融入教材，教材内容的设计未能真正体现学术英语的特点，受普通英语教材编写理念的影响仍然非常大。正是在这样的背景下，我们组织了一批长期承担学术英语教学任务的教师编写了本教材。

  本教材共8个单元，每单元由同一主题范围的课文A和课文B组成。课文材料主要选自 *Scientific American*、*New Scientist*、*Science News* 等国际科技期刊近期刊载的文章，其专业程度不超过非专业人士的理解能力，内容涉及核科学与核技术、科学语言、人工智能、计算科学、食品科学、考古、健康科学、环境与气候等多个学科领域。教材在编写过程中重点突出科学思想和学术思维，为学生的专业学习打下基础。

本教材有以下几个特点：

第一，科学素养的培养贯穿整个教材设计。科学素养是指用科学态度、科学知识和科学方法处理问题的能力。本教材在设计过程中将科学态度和科学方法融入实验描述、图表描述、引述引用、论证逻辑、文献分析等练习设计中，让学生在学习科学知识的过程中充分认识和理解科学态度和科学方法的重要性。

第二，练习的设计突出学术思维的强化。本教材旨在通过学术英语的学习，提高学生的学术英语研究能力，使其掌握并遵守国际通用的学术规范，学会用科学的思维和学术的思维阐述一个科学问题，讲好科学故事。

第三，设计多种形式的练习帮助学生读懂英文文献。本教材在编写过程中参考了国内外相关学术英语教材的内容设计，摒弃了现有教材中的普通英语思维模式，从如何做文献阅读笔记、鉴别文献写作模式、提取关键信息、把握学术话语特点、识别学术语篇组织结构等多个角度帮助学生把握语言、结构、逻辑特点；在阅读笔记、阅读技巧、学术语言等方面设计了有针对性的练习题型，使学术英语技能更加多样化，从而加深学生对文献内容的理解。

本教材配有练习答案和 PPT 课件，作为学习参考。PPT 课件中还融入了课程思政内容，以达到全面育人的目标。

本教材的编写采用主编总体设计与全面把关、编者各负其责的模式。在编写阶段，具体分工如下：陈勇负责第一、第二单元的编写和统稿工作；官芬芬负责第三、第四单元；王宗英负责第五、第七单元；李泽明负责第六、第八单元；胡步芬负责 Introduction to Academic English Reading Strategies and Skills（即学术英语阅读策略与技巧）部分，张志宾负责把关学科知识。本教材选取了近年来部分国际科技期刊的内容，我们首先要对原文作者表示最诚挚的谢意。教材在策划阶段还得到了东华理工大学教务处、国际教育学院和外国语学院的大力支持，清华大学出版社编辑刘艳女士给予了悉心的指导和帮助，在此一并致谢。

作为一项有益的尝试，全体编写人员付出了辛苦与努力，但漏误在所难免，恳请使用本教材的读者不吝赐教，以便将来再版时修正。

编者

2022 年 5 月

Introduction to Academic English Reading Strategies and Skills

Purpose of the book

The purpose of this book is to help college students develop the academic reading skills they need to effectively deal with the reading and research they will carry out in their academic study and future job. This book will particularly focus on the writing conventions of English in academic texts, which is to a certain extent different from those in general English, and provide guided instructions on how to understand the language and structure of academic texts.

Structure of the book

There are eight units in this book. Each unit has a different topic, with the purpose of familiarizing students with the styles of English for academic purposes (EAP).

There are five types of training for each unit, including fast reading, annotating skills, reading for specific information, language enhancement, and reading skills. The training particularly focuses on spotting the writer's point of view, identifying functions of the text, making notes with a mind map, describing scientific experiments, using quotes and reporting language, dealing with text-referring words, explaining words and expressions in context, etc. and provides students with helpful means to understand academic texts.

Skills for academic reading

   a. Fast reading

The purpose of fast reading is to identify what the text is about, or the main idea of the text, deciding how useful the text is for you and deciding how you will make use of the text. To be specific, you need to focus on the features of the text, such as the title, section headings, figures or graphs, first and last paragraphs, first and last sentences of intervening paragraphs, heading sentences in each paragraph, and so on. Due to different purposes, you need further information like the introduction of the writer, publication details, etc. For difficult texts, you need more detailed reading in order to identify the main idea of the text or the main points of the writer. While reading, you should do it as quickly as possible to get a general idea of the text. Remember that surveying features of the text before going into detailed reading can save time and provide important insights into the content and value of the text.

b. Annotating skills

• Identifying problem-solution pattern

In academic English, each paragraph or section has its own internal structure, which usually follows some typical pattern of organization. The most common pattern is "problem-solution". It is often used in the introduction to or the opening paragraphs of a research paper. However, it is not uncommon to find it in popular scientific writing. In the problem-solution pattern, a problem is first described, and then analyzed. The analysis may include a discussion of the process or the causes of the problem. Finally, a solution is proposed and evaluated. Thus, when reading, you are supposed to raise the following questions: What problem is described? What solution is suggested? Is there an evaluation of the solution? Note that in the problem-solution pattern, a problem may not be presented in the form of a question. Being aware of this easily recognizable pattern of organization helps you grasp the main point and identify the relationships of the ideas.

• Identifying functions of the text

One effective way of identifying functions of the text is to do it section by section, paragraph by paragraph and if necessary, sentence by sentence by annotating the text in the margin. Here are the main functions of the text:

- Background information, e.g., giving details of the overall situation, or setting the scene and looking at an existing situation, usually at the beginning of a section or text, but not always;
- General problem, i.e., a matter that involves difficulties and needs solutions;
- Exemplification, i.e., illustrating by giving examples;
- Solution, i.e., the answer to the problems, or the process of arriving at an answer;
- Definition, i.e., an exact statement or description of the nature, scope, or meaning of an important term or concept;
- Evaluation (of ideas or experimental results), i.e., judgement or analysis of solutions to certain problems;
- Explication, i.e., analyzing and developing an idea with further information;
- Implication, i.e., a possible effect or result of an action or a decision, or something that is suggested or indirectly stated;

- Viewpoint / Point of view, i.e., the writer's particular attitude or way of considering a matter;
- Summary, i.e., a brief statement that gives only the main points of something, not the details;
- Transition, i.e., terms or sentences used when a new point or idea is introduced or about to be introduced, usually happens at the beginning or end of a paragraph or section of the text;
- Conclusion, i.e., the summing-up of an argument or a text, or a judgement or decision you make when you have thought about all the information connected with the situation.

- Describing the experiment

Another effective way of identifying functions of the text is to describe the experiment, which involves the process of the experiment, experimental result(s), significance of the result(s), and the evaluation of or comment on the result(s).

- Differentiating between main ideas and supporting details

Still another effective way of identifying functions of the text is to differentiate between main ideas and supporting details. A paragraph generally contains one main idea and may have several supporting details. It is important for you to be able to extract the main ideas from a text, particularly if the text contains complex ideas and a lot of supporting points in an academic context.

c. Reading for specific information

- Using quotes

Academic texts often contain quotes from experts within the relevant field. Generally, the opinions of academics and scientists are mentioned for support and rebuttal, or comparison and contrast. Identifying quotes is helpful for you to better understand the writer's point of view.

- Understanding text-referring words

Text-referring words take their meanings from the surrounding text. They may refer back to words or ideas that have already been used, or forward to ideas that will be expanded later in the text. They include pronouns, nouns and phrases that refer to things and ideas that have already been mentioned, which avoids the writer's repeating himself/herself. It is important to be aware of the way that text-referring words clarify the progression of ideas and make the text more cohesive.

d. Language enhancement

• Understanding and using modifying language

Adjectives and adverbs are often used to modify or say more about other words in texts. They serve an important role in informing you about the writer's attitude, bias and overall writing purpose. They also perform an evaluative role so that you can critically consider the importance or relevance of certain ideas, opinions or facts.

e. Reading skills

• Identifying cohesion and coherence

Cohesion and coherence are the two basic properties of a text and the focus of text research. Cohesion refers to a close relationship based on grammar or meaning, between two parts of a sentence or a larger piece of writing. Coherence means the reasonable connection, especially in thoughts or words, in other words, the thoughts or ideas are easily understood because they are well connected. All these ideas fit together so well that they form a united whole. If the writer expresses his/her thoughts in a clear and calm way, so that other people understand what he/she is saying, he/she is coherent.

A well-written paragraph should be both coherent and cohesive. Remember to pay attention to cohesive markers, such as linking words and expressions, and any pronoun referencing or other words or phrases that link back to previous ideas. Coherence comes from the logical ordering of the content and cohesion comes from the appropriate use of linguistic features such as cohesive markers, e.g., *however*, *subsequently*, *in this respect*, *these*, etc.

• Identifying the logical order of the text

Sentences in a well-written paragraph should be in a logical order, whether from the general to the specific or vice versa, or of reasoning (claim, support, warrant, backing, rebuttal, qualifier) at a macro level, or involving the flow of sentences from one to another and the tying together of old information and new at a micro level. It is the glue that holds a piece of writing together. At the micro level, there are three effective ways: the use of transitional words and phrases, repetition of key words, and the use of reference words, all of which help to tie sentences together in a logical order and keep you on track.

• Making notes—mind map

One effective way of making notes is to draw a mind map, which is a diagrammatic method of representing ideas, with related concepts arranged around a core concept. When it comes to reading, simple "mind map" is a map made up of main ideas and the structure of the text. The efficient way to read is to recover and reconstruct the "mind map" of the writer, which is conceived and constructed before writing really begins. As an efficient reader in academic reading, you should develop the skill of making notes by drawing a mind map.

- Identifying terms and definitions

A term is a word or phrase with a specific meaning, especially one that is used in relation to a particular subject. Studying the definition or explanation of a term in academic reading is an effective way to expand vocabulary. Thus, it is necessary to look critically at various definitions or explanations of key terms given by the writer while you are researching an academic text. The wider context may be enough to help your understanding of the terms. This will also help you learn to tolerate ambiguity, which is a characteristic of good language learners.

- Identifying reporting language

Being able to identify reporting language will help you read more effectively and write academic texts such as essays, reports, and dissertations. Academic texts often contain an interesting range of reporting language. Verbs such as *highlight*, *assert* and *put forward* are often used in academic texts to report ideas and opinions. This is the way that the writer tells you, the reader, i.e., reporting what the various experts referred to in the text said or wrote about.

- Inferring meaning

When you come across a word which is unfamiliar, try to avoid automatically tapping the word into your electronic translator; develop the habit of reading on in the text to see if this helps your understanding. The following advice may be helpful.

- Look at the word in context the way it is used within the sentence.
- Think of the "root" word.
- Think about words with a similar sound or spelling that may help you.
- Try to identify synonyms because the writer may vary language through the use of synonyms.

- Reading actively

When you read, you should be doing more than simply taking in the words on the page. To understand a text well and to remember what you have read, you need to read actively. One way to read actively is to respond to the cues that the writer provides to follow the argument in the text. You may need to read a text more than once in order to identify the cues.

• Examining graphics

Displayed information such as artworks, tables of data, bar, pie and flow charts, graphs, diagrams, maps, photographs and timelines is often referred to as graphics. It has a significant purpose of decorating or breaking up a text, and should not be neglected when you are reading. For example, when you are surveying texts, graphics can quickly give you an understanding of the overall contents as they summarize or exemplify what is being described. You need to develop your capability to interpret the graphic information being displayed and to appreciate the most significant aspects of the issue.

目 录
Contents

Unit 1 Nuclear Science and Technology 1

Text A The Ultimate Battery 2
Text B Fusion of Minds 12

Unit 2 Language of Science 23

Text A Causing Trouble 24
Text B Welcome to the Fuzzy-Verse 36

Unit 3 Artificial Intelligence 49

Text A COVID-19's AI Revolution 50
Text B Hunting for New Drugs with AI 59

Unit 4 Computing Science 73

Text A Number Crunch 74
Text B Analogue Comeback 86

Unit 5 Food Science 95

Text A Making Life Look and Taste Better 96
Text B Precision Nutrition 107

Unit 6 Archeology 119

Text A The Civilization That Time Forgot 120
Text B The First Urbanites 132

Unit 7 Science of Health 145

Text A Running or Walking 146
Text B Rethinking Mental Health 158

Unit 8 Environment and Climate 171

Text A First, Protect Today's Forests 172
Text B The Promise and Pitfalls of Trees 188

UNIT 1

Nuclear Science and Technology

The Ultimate Battery

David Hanbling

① The Voyager probes, beginning what would prove to be the longest journeys ever taken by objects from Earth in 1977, have now left the solar system and Voyager 2 is sending back measurements of interstellar space. However, a crucial aspect of that success is seldom celebrated: Those probes sure do have good batteries.

② In the day-to-day grind of life, batteries never seem to last long enough. We must juice up our phones every day, laptops seem to constantly thirst for their power cables, electric cars only go so far before they fizzle out. It is enough to make you want a new type of power supply.

③ We may be edging closer to exactly that. The Voyager probes employ a weak nuclear power source that, being radioactive, is considered dangerous to use on Earth. But there is a closely related form of energy that packs even more of a punch and could work safely in an average car. It is a long shot. The last time this outlandish technology was seriously considered, 20 years ago, it ended in a broiling controversy. However, now the U.S. Army has it firmly in its sights and has conducted an experiment that might just give it a new lease of life.

④ Most of the ways we store energy involve chemistry. When we burn petrol in a car engine, we are releasing energy stored in chemical bonds. Similarly, lithium-based batteries in devices like mobile phones work by allowing charged ions to flow. But there is greater power to be had if we look beyond chemistry, inside the atom itself.

⑤ Each atom consists of a nucleus made of particles called protons and neutrons orbited by a cloud of electrons. These protons and neutrons are usually melded together in the extreme temperature and pressure inside a star, and if you delve into an atom's nucleus in the right way, you can extract some of that awesome power. The main way we do that is nuclear fission, in which a nucleus releases neutrons that can then split more atoms, causing a chain reaction that releases huge amounts of energy. That is the way the world's 440-odd nuclear energy plants work. There is also nuclear fusion, which is potentially much more powerful, but relies on smooshing together nuclei in a controlled fashion that we haven't yet mastered.

6   The Voyager probes get their power in a different way: They make use of natural radioactivity. Some atoms are unstable and spit out a chunk of matter and energy now and again. It could be a cluster of two protons and two neutrons (alpha radiation), an electron (beta radiation) or raw energy in the form of gamma rays.

7   We can't predict when a specific atom will decay in these ways, but we can say how long it will take for half of the atoms in a lump of radioactive material to do so. This is its half-life and the number can vary widely. Some radioactive materials vanish in seconds. Plutonium-238 has a half-life of 87.7 years, which is why it was chosen as the power source for Voyager 2. The plutonium dribbles out a stream of alpha particles, generating heat that is turned into electricity by the probe's three roughly suitcase-sized radioisotope thermoelectric generators.

8   Radioactivity has a bad reputation, but not all types are equal. Gamma radiation penetrates human tissue most deeply and is dangerous. Beta radiation isn't so bad. Alpha radiation doesn't get through the skin, so it is only damaging if it gets loose inside you. In fact, pacemakers were powered with well-contained radionuclide thermoelectric generators until the early 1970s.

9   The concept that the U.S. Army is eyeing up is a kind of nuclear power that blends some of the best bits of the other types—it could be powerful, safe and long-lasting. It depends on the fact that the protons and neutrons of a particular element can be clustered together in different arrangements in an atomic nucleus. These are called isomers and each has a different energy. Atoms usually reside in what is normally their most stable isomer, the ground state. Higher energy isomers tend to quickly rearrange themselves back to this state. But there are a few high-energy isomers that hang around for a long time.

Pent-up Energy

10   In 1998, Carl Collins at the University of Texas used a particle accelerator to prepare one of these stable high-energy isomers, called hafnium-178m2 (the m2 notation means this is the second isomer of hafnium-178). He then fired X-rays at its nucleus and claimed that this shifted the nucleus to its ground state, releasing a burst of gamma rays. These would be hard to tap as an energy source because they are so dangerous, but Collins saw it as proof of principle that nuclear isomers could be useful power sources. He thought they could even be used as a new type of nuclear bomb.

11   Many scientists ridiculed Collins's claims, arguing that he had to put in more energy to trigger the isomer shift than he got out. Plus, the fact that you need a particular

accelerator to make the hafnium isomer meant it could only be produced in small quantities at great expense. The episode became known as the "hafnium controversy".

12 Other high-energy isomers might get around the problems. For example, tantalum-180m occurs naturally, if rarely, in mineable tantalum deposits. Silver-108m produces beta radiation, which is less dangerous and easier to tap. None of this makes isomer power a safe bet, but the pay-off from creating an effectively unlimited energy source may make it worthwhile. A similar rationale applies to the £11.6 billion being spent on the ITER (International Thermonuclear Experimental Reactor) fusion reactor in France, even though it is intended merely as a technology demonstration and won't generate power.

13 Collins's approach was to get all the pent-up power of an isomer out in one go. But there is, in principle, a different and arguably more useful method. We have known about it for decades; it just hasn't been properly pursued.

14 Imagine you have a lump of radioactive isomer that, like hafnium-178m2, is high energy but stable. You could have this sitting safely in a container for a long time because it emits barely any radiation. When you need some power, you convert a small amount of it into its ground state, which is less stable and begins to radioactively decay quickly. This gives you a generator akin to the one in Voyager 2, but which can be cranked up in power at will.

15 James Carroll at the U.S. Army Research Laboratory in Adelphi, Maryland, has been investigating whether interconverting isomers in this way is possible. One potential way to do it, first proposed in 1976, involves firing an electron at an isomer and it being absorbed into an orbit around the nucleus. This prompts the protons and neutrons to rearrange. It is called nuclear excitation by electron capture (NEEC).

16 Carroll and his team used a particle accelerator at Argonne National Laboratory near Chicago to create a beam of molybdenum-93m atoms, with a half-life of about 7 hours. This beam was travelling at about 10 percent of the speed of light, fast enough to strip away some of the atoms' electrons. It was then smashed into a target, which injected electrons back into the nuclei, while nudging them into a less stable isomer. This isomer decayed so quickly that the researchers couldn't observe it. But they inferred it was created by the gamma rays it produced. The work, published in 2018, is the first time NEEC had been demonstrated.

17 "The experiment has been a significant step forward, but the jury is out regarding whether or not it is a breakthrough for NEEC," says Philip Walker, who studies nuclear isomer physics at the University of Surrey, U.K. This is largely because there is a dispute

over how much energy can be wrung out of isomers. Carroll's figures suggest that the process could produce 5 joules of energy for every joule put in, assuming 1 percent of atoms undergo NEEC.

18   Adriana Pálffy at the Max Planck Institute for Nuclear Physics in Heidelberg, Germany, isn't so sure. Her calculations suggest that a billion times fewer atoms should be depleted through radioactive decay. If true, that raises questions about where the energy that Carroll saw is coming from. "The experimental results may be valid, but their interpretation of what happened in the process cannot be correct," says Pálffy.

19   Carroll admits that isomers are far from being of practical use as batteries. But the arguments that applied after Collins's work still apply: There are other isomers that could be more accessible and easier to harness. The trouble is that the exact properties of isomers are tough to calculate, and we won't know how suitable they are until we try them.

20   At the moment, there is no sense of how isomer shifting could be done at a smaller scale than in a particle accelerator. Still, there is ample drive to get isomer batteries to work because they would pack gigantic amounts of energy into a small volume. "Isomers can store energy with a capacity of up to over gigajoules per gram," says Rzadkiewicz. That's a million times more than lithium-ion batteries, and tens of thousands of times more than petrol.

Risk and Reward

21   Carroll says an uncrewed army vehicle known as a SMET, used to carry soldiers' equipment, could run for 163 days on 1 kilogram of americium-242m. The current version runs for three days on 20 litres of petrol. Drones or robot submarines could also be given isomer energy sources. It is easy to see why the Army is interested.

22   Safety is going to be a concern for anything with "nuclear" in its name, and if isomer power produces gamma rays, that will preclude its use. But if isomers can be found that emit beta or alpha particles, it could be feasible. Plenty of people work close to stores of materials used for radiotherapy and diagnostics. "The amounts of radioactive material needed for a battery are probably less than the material routinely shipped around hospitals," says Patrick Regan at the University of Surrey.

23   Isomer power is the longest of long shots. But then many of our greatest achievements seemed that way at the beginning. When the space race began, who would have thought that, just decades later, we would have sent a probe beyond the edge of the solar system? (*New Scientist*, September 26, 2020)

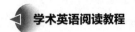

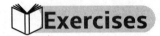

I Fast reading

Task 1 Tick (√) the statement that most closely reflects the writer's point of view.

(　) A. Nuclear fusion is the future of energy source.

(　) B. A new type of nuclear energy resource—high-energy isomers—could create long-lasting batteries.

(　) C. The power source of Voyager probes is unique and has aroused interest of researchers.

(　) D. Isomers are hard to harness as the exact properties of isomers could not be calculated.

II Annotating skills

Task 2 Find texts that describe experiments and analyze them in detail. An example has been given for you. Then find two more experiments from Text A.

Example:

In 1998, Carl Collins at the University of Texas used a particle accelerator to prepare one of these stable high-energy isomers, called hafnium-178m2 (the m2 notation means this is the second isomer of hafnium-178). He then fired X-rays at its nucleus and claimed that this shifted the nucleus to its ground state, releasing a burst of gamma rays. These would be hard to tap as an energy source because they are so dangerous, but Collins saw it as a proof of principle that nuclear isomers could be useful power sources. He thought they could even be used as a new type of nuclear bomb.

Process of the experiment: In 1998, Carl Collins <u>used</u> a particle accelerator to <u>prepare</u> hafnium-178m2. He <u>then fired</u> X-rays at its nucleus.

UNIT 1 Nuclear Science and Technology

Result: He claimed that this shifted the nucleus to its ground state, releasing a burst of gamma rays.

Significance: A proof of principle that nuclear isomers could be useful power sources and could even be used as a new type of nuclear bomb.

Evaluation: First, gamma rays would be hard to tap as an energy source because they are very dangerous. Second, he had to put in more energy to trigger the isomer shift than he got out. Third, energy could only be produced in small quantities at great expense.

1. _____
_____
_____
_____
_____.

Process of the experiment: _____
_____.

Result: _____
_____.

Significance: _____
_____.

Evaluation: _____
_____.

2. _____
_____
_____
_____
_____.

Process of the experiment: _____
_____.

Result: _____
_____.

Significance: _____
_____.

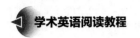

Evaluation: _____

_____.

III Reading for specific information

Task 3 Read Text A carefully, but as fast as you can. Try to answer as many questions as you can without referring to the text.

1. When did the Voyager probes begin their space journeys?

2. Which aspect of the Voyager probes' success is seldom mentioned?

3. In what way is energy stored in petrol?

4. What is the way that the world's nuclear power plants work?

5. Why do we fail to get steady energy from nuclear fusion?

6. How do the Voyager probes get their power?

7. What is the half-life of Plutonium-238?

8. Which is the most harmful to our health, gamma radiation, beta radiation or alpha radiation?

9. What isomers did Carl Collins experiment with?

10. When has NEEC been demonstrated for the first time?

Task 4 Read the text and try to find the text-referring words in the table. Note down the idea or word(s) that each one refers to. The first one has been done for you.

Text-referring word(s)	Refers to...	Paragraph
However, a crucial aspect of *that* success is seldom celebrated	the Voyager probes, which have taken the longest journeys ever from Earth in 1977, have now left the solar system and Voyager 2 is sending back information.	1

UNIT 1 Nuclear Science and Technology

(Continued)

Text-referring word(s)	Refers to...	Paragraph
We may be edging closer to exactly *that*		3
That is the way the world's 440-odd nuclear energy plants work		5
We can't predict when a specific atom will decay in *these* ways		7
These are called isomers and each has a different energy		9
Other high-energy isomers might get around *the problems*		12
Whether interconverting isomers in *this way* is possible		15

IV Language enhancement

Task 5 Locate the phrases in the text and complete the table below by explaining the meaning of each italicized word in your own words. Pay attention to the writer's choice of the adjective or adverb for emphasis. The first one has been done for you.

Phrase	Meaning	Paragraph
crucial aspect	extremely important	1
constantly thirst		2
closely related		3
seriously considered		3
extreme temperature		5
awesome power		5

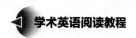

(Continued)

Phrase	Meaning	Paragraph
arguably more useful method		13
properly pursued		13
practical use		19
gigantic amounts		20

Task 6 Locate the words or phrases in the text and try to work out their meanings in context. Think about how the writer uses these words and phrases below and the effect the writer's use of language has on the reader. The first one has been done for you.

Word or phrase	Meaning	Paragraph
day-to-day grind of life	routine tasks or activities that are boring and take up a lot of time and effort	2
juice up		2
fizzle out		2
pack a punch		3
give it a new lease of life		3
a cloud of electrons		5
smoosh together		5
half-life		7
get loose		8
eye up		9
tap		10
proof of principle		10
pent-up		13

UNIT 1 Nuclear Science and Technology

(Continued)

Word or phrase	Meaning	Paragraph
the jury is out		17
the longest of long shots		23

V Reading skills: Cohesion and coherence

Task 7 Find examples of cohesion and coherence in Text A and complete the flow chart below.

Example 1

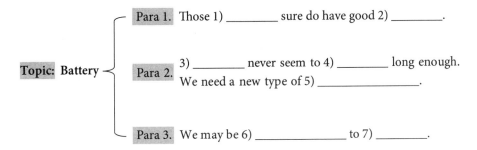

Example 2

Para. 4. Most of the ways we 1) _____ energy… Similarly, … But there is 2) _____ power… inside the 3) ____ itself.

Para. 5. Each 4) _____ consists of… the main way… is nuclear 5) _____ … There is also nuclear 6) _____ …

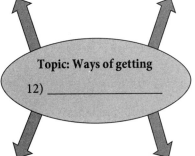

Para. 6. The Voyager probes get power in a 7) _____ way: using natural radioactivity—alpha, 8) _____, gamma.

Para. 7. 9) _____ in these ways; this is the 10) _____ and the 11) _____ varies widely.

Example 3

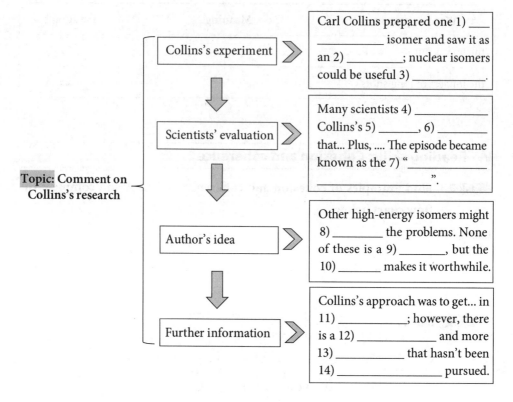

Text B

Fusion of Minds

Abigail Beall

1 The big joke about sustainable nuclear fusion is that it has always been 30 years away. Like any joke, it contains a kernel of truth. The dream of harnessing the reaction that powers the sun was big news in the 1950s, just around the corner in the 1980s, and the hottest bet of the past decade.

2 But time is running out. Our demand for energy is burning up the planet, depleting its resources and risking damaging Earth beyond repair. Wind, solar and tidal energy provide some relief, but they are limited and unpredictable. Nuclear fission comes with the dangers of reactor meltdowns and radioactive waste, while hydropower can be ecologically disruptive. Fusion, on the other hand, could provide almost limitless energy without releasing carbon dioxide or producing radioactive waste. It is the dream power source. The perennial question is: Can we make it a reality?

UNIT **1** Nuclear Science and Technology

3   Perhaps now, finally, we can. That isn't just because of the myriad fusion start-ups increasingly sensing a lucrative market opportunity just around the corner and challenging the primacy of the traditional big-beast projects, or just because of innovative approaches, materials and technologies that are fuelling an optimism that we can at last master fusion's fiendish complexities. It is also because of the entrance of a new player, one that could change the rules of the game: artificial intelligence. In the right hands, it might make the next 30 years fly by.

4   Nuclear fusion is the most widespread source of energy in the universe, and one of the most efficient: Just a few grams of fuel release the same energy as several tonnes of coal. These vast quantities of energy have their origins in something vanishingly small: the nucleus of an atom. Consisting of positively charged protons and neutral neutrons orbited by negatively charged electrons, the nucleus makes up the bulk of an atom's mass.

5   When two or more small atomic nuclei come into contact, they can, under certain circumstances, merge to form larger nuclei, releasing huge amounts of energy in the process. On a gargantuan scale, this is what takes place within the core of stars like our sun, giving them the power they need to shine for billions of years.

6   Fusion's extraordinary potential has been tantalizing scientists for decades, but remains difficult to realise on Earth. It requires the creation of a "plasma" of naked atomic nuclei at huge temperatures and densities—something that is both difficult to achieve and difficult to control.

7   At present, the most popular approach is to use what is called a magnetic confinement fusion device. In fusion's early days in the 1950s, the favoured design was a kinked doughnut shape known as a stellarator. These machines created complex magnetic fields that could theoretically hold a charged plasma steady, but their twisted shape made them tricky to build.

8   By the 1970s, interest had turned to simpler designs: vast hollow rings called tokamaks in which trapped plasma is heated to hundreds of millions of degrees. The forces required to keep such a plasma in place can only be generated by powerful superconducting magnets cooled to close to absolute zero, creating the sharpest temperature gradients in the known universe.

9   These magnetic confinement devices have had a few successes over the years. In 1997, the Joint European Torus (JET) near Oxford, U.K., set the world record for the amount of energy created in a fusion reaction, producing 16 megawatts of fusion energy from an input of 24 megawatts. This is the closest anyone has got to breaking even—

getting as much energy out as that pumped in—but the reaction lasted for only a few hundredths of a second.

10   Back then, break-even seemed around the corner, but strange instabilities appeared in JET's plasma that worked to cool down its centre and stymie the plans. Now, after years of upgrades and changes in design and materials, the reactor is back. In November 2020, JET is set to power its first fusion reaction in more than 20 years, aiming to beat its previous energy record and sustain the reaction for longer.

11   Meanwhile, other players have been getting in on the act. In 2018, China's Experimental Advanced Superconducting Tokamak (EAST) sustained a plasma at temperatures of 15 million °C for 100 seconds, the longest confinement time yet.

12   EAST plans to start operating again in 2020, but is comparatively small fry. The heavily backed favourite in the race is the huge International Thermonuclear Experimental Reactor, or ITER. Founded in 1985 as a collaboration between 31 nations including China, the U.S., Russia and the European Union, ITER was originally expected to start experiments in 2016, but design challenges mean it is likely to remain under construction in France until 2025. "ITER is a first-of-a-kind facility," says Howard Wilson at the University of York, U.K. "It will take 10 years to learn how to bring it up to its full performance."

13   ITER currently aims to begin fusion reactions in 2035, and it has big goals: pushing beyond break-even to produce 10 times as much power as goes in. Despite the delays, there is confidence that ITER will achieve this. "The question now is, do we have the technology to make a commercially viable power plant?" asks Simon Pinches, head of the plasma physics division at ITER.

14   Even if ITER achieves its goals, its journey will be far from over. The reactor isn't set up to capture the energy it produces as electricity. Instead, the idea is that it will pave the way for demonstration power plants down the line. One is the China Fusion Engineering Test Reactor (CFETR), a follow-up tokamak to EAST three times the size, which is expected to be built in the late 2020s.

15   But with climate change looming ever larger, the need to find alternatives to fossil fuels has become more urgent. That has coincided with a flurry of innovation across the fusion industry, aiming to make cheap, sustainable reactors a reality within years, not decades. The most important has been the discovery of superconductors that work at higher temperatures, and so can generate strong magnetic fields with less dramatic refrigeration. Such superconductors allowed magnets to become smaller, and tokamaks to be more compact.

16   Other recent breakthroughs in technology, ranging from improved construction techniques to robotic systems that can inspect and maintain parts of the reactor, have made it cheaper to get into the fusion business. "It's gone from being a purely academic activity that only government-funded research labs can fund, to something that private individuals are prepared to invest in," says Pinches.

17   This has sparked a race between private companies to be the first to achieve sustainable fusion. One prominent competitor aiming to exploit the same tokamak concepts as JET, ITER and EAST is Commonwealth Fusion Systems. As a spin-off from the Massachusetts Institute of Technology, it is partly funded by billionaires and is aiming to produce a reactor within the next 10 years. Other challengers, like Windridge's Tokamak Energy, are also aiming to provide power to the grid by 2030.

18   Some are wary of promises given by private companies. "Even with those companies which have been around for a longer time, it's still the promise of a reactor in 10 years from now," says Tony Donné, programme manager for EUROfusion, the consortium in charge of JET. Partly, these timescales are given to keep investors happy. "I'm sceptical that they will deliver a fusion reactor much faster than we have," says Donné. "If the community thought there was an easier way of doing it, they'd be doing that," says Pinches.

19   Whether public or private, everyone designing tokamaks is facing the same problems. Chief among them is how to handle instabilities in the plasma. When hot plasma is contained within the magnetic fields of a tokamak, it behaves weirdly. Sometimes small ripples appear like on the surface of a lake, while at others huge tidal waves send the plasma shooting towards the reactor walls. It is enough for some people to seek alternatives to the magnetic confinement technique, which depends on the plasma remaining stable for a long time.

20   Starting in the 1980s, some researchers looking for such alternatives dived into the past, dusting off the long-abandoned stellarators. Their more complex design generated magnetic field patterns capable of stabilizing the plasma, says Amitava Bhattacharjee at Princeton University. What's more, increases in computing power meant it was becoming possible to model how plasma behaved within their more complex configurations, and so potentially created more effective designs. "This produced a renaissance in stellarator research," says Bhattacharjee. At the same time, new materials and construction methods mean building a stellarator has never been easier.

21   And while stellarators still lag decades behind tokamaks, they are starting to catch up. In 2015, Wendelstein 7-X, the largest stellarator in the world, was switched on at the

Max Planck Institute for Plasma Physics in Greifswald, Germany, and is gearing up to maintain a plasma for 30 minutes, with this milestone expected in 2021. After that, the aim will be to start fusion.

22   It is still a hugely complex, time-consuming business trying to work out how best to build a fusion reactor, however. "Finding the optimum design of stellarators typically requires playing around with about 50 parameters until the best design is arrived at," says Bhattacharjee. Plasma instabilities can plague any reactor design, and understanding the complex behaviour involved requires a lot of data and time. "A fully integrated predictive simulation for ITER could take many weeks to run at present," says Pinches.

23   That is why, over the past few years, plasma physicists have been turning to a new partner to help haul a sustainable reactor design over the finishing line: machine minds. "Artificial intelligence can give us much greater speed and a much deeper exploration of the range of possibilities," says Bhattacharjee.

24   TAE Technologies, a California-based fusion research company, has had a partnership with Google's DeepMind AI set-up since 2014, while Canada's General Fusion is working with Microsoft. Improvements are already emerging, says David Ewing at TAE, particularly with regard to modelling how the plasma reacts to different configurations of temperature, density and magnetic field. "Previous to our advancements in machine learning, optimizing the performance for a particular experiment set-up could take well over a month," says Ewing. "These can now be achieved within hours."

25   Key to this speed-up is AI's ability to recognize patterns and make predictions about future behaviour. You can't put a thermometer inside a tokamak to understand its workings, so the temperature has to be inferred from other properties, like how much light is coming out. This can be a difficult task for a human researcher, but an AI trained on mountainous data sets can dramatically cut the time it takes—and also up the efficiency. In 2019, a team at Princeton paired the U.S.'s fastest supercomputer with a neural network to predict plasma disruptions with an unprecedented 95 percent accuracy.

26   Artificial intelligence could also be a rocket booster for ITER, too. "For some tasks, like modelling the consequences of small ripples in the plasma, AI has already made the job 10 million times faster," says Pinches. Now the key is to boost the speed of the whole simulation, allowing researchers to predict problems and avoid them without needing to run the experiment.

27　Such innovations, and the speed at which they are now happening, is bringing a new optimism that fusion's time could, finally, be nearing. "In the last decade, we've seen exponential progress in the science," says Ewing. "That, coupled with the emergence of critical support technologies like AI, has now created the proper tool chest to bring us to the cusp of a breakthrough." The old joke about fusion hasn't dated, but this time its backers may have the last laugh. (*New Scientist*, June 13, 2020)

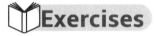

I　Fast reading

Task 1　Tick (√) the statement that most closely reflects the writer's point of view.

(　) A. Fusion start-ups have joined the race for nuclear fusion and may make it possible.

(　) B. New materials and technologies may help us master the complexities of nuclear fusion.

(　) C. Artificial intelligence could bring us to the cusp of a breakthrough and speed up the realization of nuclear fusion.

(　) D. In this race for nuclear fusion, stellarators are more promising than tokamaks.

II　Annotating skills

Task 2　Identify which functions the following paragraphs of the text have, complete the table below using the annotations you have made, and find key information in relevant paragraphs as extra comment. The first one has been done for you.

- background information
- general problem
- solution
- exemplification
- cause
- explication
- implication
- evaluation
- viewpoint

- definition
- transition
- summary
- comparison & contrast
- conclusion

Paragraph(s)	Function	Extra comment
1–2	general problem	Fusion power has been tantalizing for decades. There is finally an answer to the old question.
3		
4–5		
6–14		
15–26		
2, 18, 22		
16–26		

III Reading for specific information

Task 3 Read Text B carefully, but as fast as you can. Try to answer as many questions as you can without referring to the text.

1. When did the fusion power first attract the attention of the public?

2. Why do we urgently need new types of energy like fusion power?

3. What are the major problems of fission power?

4. What are the overwhelming advantages of the fusion power?

5. What is a nucleus made up of?

6. Why is it so difficult to realize nuclear fusion?

7. When was the stellarator first designed?

8. When was the tokamak first designed?

9. How long did the fusion reaction of JET last in 1997?

UNIT **1** Nuclear Science and Technology

10. How long did the fusion reaction of China's EAST last?

11. When could ITER start experiments?

12. What is ITER's big goal?

13. What is the relationship between EAST and CFETR?

14. What is the common problem that every tokamak designer has to cope with?

15. In what way could AI help to speed up the sustainable reactor design?

Task 4 Academic texts often contain quotes from experts within the relevant field. In Text B, the opinions of a number of experts are mentioned. Read the opinions below. Then scan the text for information, matching each opinion to the relevant expert. The first one has been done for you.

Howard Wilson   Simon Pinches   Tony Donné   Amitava Bhattacharjee   David Ewing

1. It will take 10 years for us to learn to make full use of the brand-new facility of ITER.
   __Howard Wilson__

2. Even if we could achieve break-even, we still do not have the technology to construct a commercially viable fusion power plant at present. _____

3. It seems doubtful that private companies could be faster than the government-funded labs in making a fusion reactor. _____

4. The modern stellarator's magnetic field patterns of a more complex design could stabilize the plasma. _____

5. Private companies have entered the fusion business which used to be a purely academic activity funded exclusively by government. _____

6. Increasing computing power, especially artificial intelligence, could help to model the behavior of plasma in more complex configurations and give impetus for stellarator research.
   _____

19

7. About 50 parameters are involved in the optimum design of stellarators, so a fully integrated predictive simulation for ITER could take weeks to run currently. _____

8. The joint efforts of fusion research companies and AI giants have greatly improved the modelling of how the plasma reacts to different configurations of temperature, density and magnetic field, so fusion's time is nearing more than ever before. _____

IV Language enhancement

Task 5 Locate the phrases in the text and complete the table below by explaining the meaning of each italicized word in your own words. Pay attention to the writer's choice of the adjective or adverb for emphasis. The first one has been done for you.

Phrase	Meaning	Paragraph
sustainable nuclear fusion	able to be maintained at a certain rate or level, involving the use of the energy in a way that does not harm the environment	1
radioactive waste		2
ecologically disruptive		2
perennial question		2
lucrative market		3
fiendish complexities		3
vanishingly small		4
positively/negatively charged		4
gargantuan scale		5
absolute zero		8
commercially viable		13
prominent competitor		17

UNIT **1** Nuclear Science and Technology

(Continued)

Phrase	Meaning	Paragraph
optimum design		22
dramatically cut		25
exponential progress		27

Task 6 Locate the words or phrases in the text and try to work out their meanings in context. Think about how the writer uses these words and phrases below and the effect the writer's choice of language has on the reader. The first one has been done for you.

Word or phrase	Meaning	Paragraph
a kernel of truth	a small element of the truth	1
around the corner		1
reactor meltdown		2
start-up		3
big-beast project		3
tantalize		6
tricky		7
gradient		8
break even		9
small fry		12
demonstration power plant		14
down the line		14
spin-off		17

V Reading skills: Making notes—mind map

Task 7 Read Paragraphs 6–27 of Text B and complete the mind map below. You may use some of the information in the mind map to write the first draft of your summary.

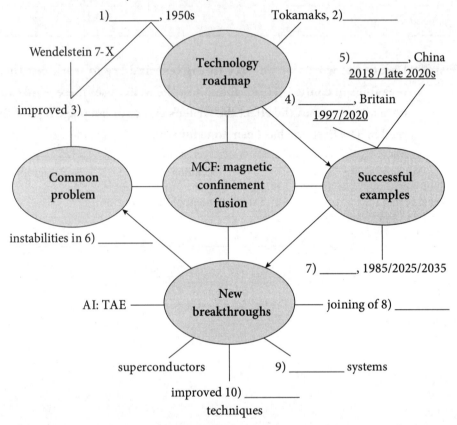

UNIT 2

Language of Science

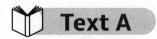

Causing Trouble

Ciarán Gilligan-Lee

1   In the mid-1990s, an algorithm trained on hospital admission data made a surprising prediction. It said that people who presented with pneumonia were more likely to survive if they also had asthma. This flew in the face of all medical knowledge, which said that asthmatic patients were at increased risk from the disease. Yet the data gathered from multiple hospitals was indisputable: If you had asthma, your chances were better. What was going on?

2   It turned out that the algorithm had missed a crucial piece of the puzzle. Doctors treating pneumonia patients with asthma were passing them straight to the intensive care unit, where the aggressive treatment significantly reduced their risk of dying from pneumonia. It was a case of cause and effect being hopelessly entangled. Fortunately, no changes were rolled out on the basis of the algorithm.

3   Unweaving the true connection between cause and effect is crucial for modern-day science. It underpins everything from the development of medication to the design of infrastructure and even our understanding of the laws of physics. But for well over a century, scientists have lacked the tools to get it right. Not only has the difference between cause and effect often been impossible to work out from data alone, but we have struggled to reliably distinguish causal links from coincidence.

4   Now, mathematical work could fix that for good, giving science the causal language that it desperately needs. This has far-ranging applications in our data-rich age, from drug discovery to medical diagnosis, and may be the essential tool to resolve this fatal flaw.

5   A mantra most scientists can recite in their sleep is that correlation doesn't imply causation. A simple example illustrates why. Data from seaside towns tells us that the more ice creams are sold on a day, the more bathers are attacked by sharks. Does this mean that ice cream vendors should be shut down in the interests of public safety? Probably not. A more sensible conclusion is that the two trends are likely to be consequences of an underlying third factor: more people on the beach. In that case, the rise in ice cream sales and shark attacks would both be caused by the rise in beachgoers, but only correlated to each other.

What's Going On?

6 This analysis seems simple enough. The trouble is that the data alone can't point us in the right direction. We need some external knowledge—in this case, that a surge in people enjoying the beach on a hot day can adequately explain both trends—to correctly distinguish correlation from causation. As the data at hand gets more complicated and less familiar, however, our ability to distinguish between the two falls short.

7 These subtleties were lost on some of the early pioneers of statistics. One notable offender was Karl Pearson, an English mathematician and prominent eugenicist of the early 1900s. Pearson believed the mathematics of correlation was the true grammar of science, with causation being only a special case of correlation, rather than a separate analytical concept. The statistical tools he developed remain part of the bedrock of scientific practice, and are taught in every undergraduate statistics class. As a result, for over a century, many scientific discoveries have been based on flimsy correlation rather than firm causation. This has implications far beyond the seaside. Data and correlation can tell you which of two treatments led patients to recover faster, but not why. They also can't tell you how to make treatments better, or even what to prescribe a given individual.

8 "If you want to actually cure a disease, or make it less likely that someone gets a disease, you need to have a causal understanding," says Jonas Peters at the University of Copenhagen in Denmark. "The importance of understanding causality can't be overstated," says Elias Bareinboim at Columbia University in New York. "I don't think there is any way of doing science without causality," he says. "It is the code running the system."

9 At the same time, science is poorly equipped to deal with questions of cause and effect. Since Galileo, modern science has been communicated using the language of algebra and equations. Physicists can write an equation describing the relationship between atmospheric pressure and the reading on a barometer, but this equation says nothing about whether it is pressure that causes the barometer reading or vice versa. The language of algebra is completely agnostic to the question of which came first.

10 In the early 1990s, dissatisfied with this state of affairs, Judea Pearl at the University of California, Los Angeles, set out to give science the causal language it desperately needed. His solution was to introduce a new mathematical language of "doing", allowing us to distinguish between cause and effect. If I "do" by intervening to force pressure to change, then the reading on the barometer will shift. But if I "do" a change in the barometer reading, the pressure doesn't alter as a consequence. Intervening on the cause will change the effect, but any intervention on the effect won't change the cause.

11 To convey this in mathematical terms, Pearl invented a new operation to sit alongside addition, subtraction and the others. Just like the other operators, his "do operator" can manipulate variables—like the number of ice creams sold—in specific ways. Whereas addition combines the value of two or more variables, the do operator sets a variable to a specific value, irrespective of anything else.

12 To see why this is needed, let's head back to the seaside. If we wanted to establish the true relationship between ice cream eating and shark attacks, the scientific best practice would be to carry out a randomized controlled trial. This would involve randomly assigning beachgoers into two subgroups of equal size. One group would be given ice creams and the other wouldn't. Both would then be let loose in shark-infested waters, and the number of shark attacks on each group compared.

13 The composition of the subgroups is random, so all other potentially confounding factors, such as age, height and tastiness of flesh, are controlled for. Any remaining correlation can be explained only if there is a direct causal relationship between eating ice cream and being attacked by a shark. By changing ice cream consumption alone, and keeping everything else fixed, any corresponding change in shark attacks must be due to eating ice cream, as it is the only variable that changed.

14 Pearl's great insight was to show that with the do operator you could effectively simulate a randomized controlled trial using only observational data and extract causal connections. This was a game changer, because performing real-world randomized controlled trials can be expensive and complicated, not to mention unethical. To perform a controlled trial to examine the link between pneumonia and asthma, for example, half the group would have to be infected with pneumonia.

15 The work won Pearl the Turing Award in 2011—the computer science equivalent of a Nobel prize—and formed the foundations of what has come to be known as the theory of causal inference.

16 Besides putting science on a firmer causal footing, this mathematical framework is helping to solve problems in many disciplines, says Bareinboim, chief among which is the replication crisis that has plagued medicine and the social sciences. In the past decade, doubts have arisen about many headline-grabbing studies in these fields—from the noting that maths problems are easier for students to solve if written in a fuzzy font to the idea that willpower is a finite, exhaustible resource—because the results of their underlying experiments couldn't be replicated. In 2015, a massive replicability study in

psychology found that results of 60 percent of studies couldn't be reproduced, casting a vast shadow across the discipline.

17   Bareinboim believes causal inference could help clear these problems up. In many cases, he says, the original tests were susceptible to confounding factors that the experimenters may have been unaware of, and subsequent replication attempts might have dragged new causal relationships into the mix. One classic example concerns the effect of happiness on economic decisions, which was originally measured by showing participants footage of U.S. comedian Robin Williams. By the time the replication experiment was conducted, Williams had died, potentially skewing the participants' response. In addition, the subjects in the original study were from the U.S., but those in the replication one were British. By not controlling for such confounding effects, the replication study cannot legitimately comment on the original finding.

18   The applications extend well beyond science. "As soon as you're looking to improve decision-making, you want to understand cause and effect. Which is, if I were to do this, how would the world change?" says Suchi Saria at Johns Hopkins University in Maryland. Economists in particular were early to the party, realizing that many of the problems they wished to solve required a causal toolkit.

19   Such tools could determine the effects of specific policies, such as whether an increased tax on cigarettes reduces the health impacts of smoking. For such a complicated issue, however, Pearl's mathematical tools become incredibly challenging. The relationship between smoking and health is influenced by a panoply of confounding factors, including age, sex, diet, family history, occupation and years of education. To home in on the causal connection we care about, we can look only at parts of the data where the other factors are constant. But for each confounding variable we control for, the corresponding data set gets smaller. Eventually, we are left with so little data that no robust conclusions can be drawn at all.

20   To overcome these difficulties, Susan Athey at Stanford University in California and her colleagues have developed techniques to approximate Pearl's methods while still holding on to as much data as possible. They aren't alone. Tools of this kind are also having a big impact in healthcare, an area where understanding cause and effect can be life-saving. Knowing that a disease is highly correlated with certain symptoms, or that a drug is highly correlated with recovery, isn't enough, and basing medical decisions on such information can be dangerous.

21   Saria is using causal inference to create tools to help doctors make decisions by comparing the effect of different medical actions. However, working with medical data comes with challenges. "We may be reflecting back biases that are not the true

underlying phenomena in nature," she says. For example, unequal access to treatment means that the U.S. spends less money caring for black patients than for white patients. Some algorithms conclude from such data that black patients are healthier than equally sick white patients, which is patently false.

22 For Kira Radinsky at the Technion-Israel Institute of Technology, causal understanding is key to a more equitable health system. "If you don't understand the causal processes, you are susceptible to bias in the data," she says. "As soon as you do understand them, you can clean out the bias."

23 This highlights one problem that causal inference can't solve. Before Pearl's techniques can be employed, the causal relationships need to be known. Left to analyse shark attack and ice cream sales data, for example, they wouldn't be able to determine the connection between the two without knowing that an increase in beachgoers could explain both trends.

24 To quantitatively compute the effect of treating someone's symptoms with a certain drug, we need to know that a causal relationship between that drug and those symptoms exists. The standard approach to this is to find out from experts on the subject.

25 But getting this causal knowledge from experts can be difficult and takes time, says Radinsky. The approach she and her collaborators have taken to streamline this process is to mine causal relationships from medical papers that actually verified their existence through experiments. By applying this causal knowledge to drug repurposing—using existing medicines in new ways—they have already found new treatments for hypertension and diabetes.

Learning from the Data

26 This is a fruitful and powerful approach, but not every field has a large collection of online research papers with proven causal links just waiting to be exploited. This has led researchers in other disciplines to wonder if causal relationships could be discovered from purely observational data. The age-old difficulty of distinguishing correlation from causation would seem to rule this out. Yet a new generation of researchers bold enough to investigate the problem is starting to realise that it might not be as impossible as it sounds.

27 One approach gaining ground involves looking for patterns that hold true regardless of circumstances. Increased atmospheric pressure always causes a barometer reading to change, for example, regardless of whether you are in London or New York, on Earth or Mars. Likewise, physicians in different hospitals or countries may differ in how they treat people, but the underlying causal relationships between diseases and symptoms don't vary. The key idea behind new work being led by Peters and others is

that his consistency can act as a signature of the underlying causal process, allowing Pearl's tools to be deployed.

28   To put this principle to the test, he and his colleagues dived into a complex sociological question: the true causes of a country's total fertility rate. These rates vary dramatically around the world, and understanding the factors determining them could be a boon for governments seeking to support their populations. By looking for consistent patterns in data from multiple countries, Peters and his colleagues found that mortality rates of young children were important drivers of fertility rates, a finding that tallied with previous studies from around the world. "When child mortality is high, families tend to have more children, even if none of their own children has died," says Adrian Raftery, a sociologist and statistician at the University of Washington in Seattle. "This may be proactive, to try to make sure that they do have a family."

29   Bareinboim is very excited about the group's ability to obtain causal insights from observational data alone. "When that work came along, it was amazing," he says. Peters and his collaborators are now using the invariance principle to paint a causal picture of biosphere and atmosphere interactions, with potentially dramatic consequences for our understanding of climate change.

30   But like Pearson's statistical analysis over a century ago, it is not a silver bullet. To truly disentangle cause, effect and correlation, scientists will always need extra contextual information. Without knowing how beachgoers behave, for instance, or how doctors treat people with pneumonia if they have asthma, no analysis in the world could correctly parse even the largest data set. "The problem is the data-generating process," says Athey, "not the limits of our brains." (*New Scientist*, April 25, 2020)

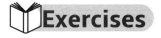

Exercises

I   Fast reading

Task 1   Tick (√) the statement that accurately explains the meaning of the title "Causing Trouble".

(   ) A. Bringing about a problem, or something bad or unpleasant

(   ) B. Problem of cause and effect being entangled

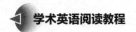

Task 2 Tick (√) the statement that most closely reflects the writer's point of view.

(　) A. Instead of a separate analytical concept, causation is only a special case of correlation.

(　) B. Scientists have already obtained their own causal language.

(　) C. Mathematics of correlation is the true grammar of science.

(　) D. To distinguish correlation from causation, scientists need both the extra contextual information and the data-generating process.

II Annotating skills

Task 3 In Text A, the writer has made full use of the problem-solution pattern. Read the text carefully and complete the table below using the annotations you have made.

Paragraph(s)	Annotation: Problem and solution
9	**Problem:** 1) _____ could not tell 2) _____ from effect; the language of 3) _____ is completely 4) _____ to the question of which came 5) _____.
10–18	**Solution:** Judea Pearl's new mathematical language of 6) "_____", or 7) "_____".
19	**New problem:** Pearl's 8) _____ become incredibly 9) _____ when they are applied to 10) _____.
20–21	**Solution:** Susan Athey and her colleagues' techniques of 11) _____ Pearl's methods while still 12) _____ as much 13) _____ as possible; Saria's tools based on 14) _____.
21	**New problem:** Challenges from 15) _____.
22–24	**Solution:** Causal understanding is the key to 16) _____ in the 17) _____ and 18) _____ need to be known before we employ 19) _____.

(Continued)

Paragraph(s)	Annotation: Problem and solution
25	**New problem:** Getting this 20) _____ from 21) _____ can be difficult and takes time.
25	**Solution:** Radinsky and her collaborators' approach of 22) _____ causal relationships from 23) _____ .
26	**New problem:** Not every field has a large 24) _____ of online research papers with 25) _____ waiting to be 26) _____ .
27	**Solution:** Looking for 27) _____ that hold 28) _____ regardless of 29) _____ .

III Reading for specific information

Task 4 Read Text A carefully, but as fast as you can. Try to answer as many questions as you can without referring to the text.

1. What was the medical knowledge that flew in the face of the results obtained from hospital admission data?

2. What is the fundamental cause of the puzzle mentioned in Paragraph 2?

3. What could resolve the flaw in the true connection between cause and effect according to the writer?

4. Apart from the data itself, what else do we need to distinguish correlation from causation?

5. What is Pearson's point of view on correlation and causation?

6. What is the writer's comment on Pearson's point of view?

7. Whom does the writer quote to support his own argument?

8. What was Pearl's solution to the causation problem?

9. What is the significance of Pearl's solution?

10. What did Susan Athey and her colleagues do to improve Pearl's methods?

11. What is exactly the problem that causal inference cannot solve?

12. What do scientists need to truly disentangle cause, effect and correlation?

Task 5 Read the text and try to find the text-referring words listed in the table. Note down the idea or word(s) that each one refers to. The first one has been done for you.

Text-referring word(s)	Refers to...	Paragraph
Now, mathematical work could fix *that* for good	It refers to the last sentence of Para. 3: Not only has the difference between cause and effect often been impossible to work out from data alone, but we have struggled to reliably distinguish causal links from coincidence.	4
This analysis seems simple enough		6
In the early 1990s, dissatisfied with *this state of affairs*		10
To convey *this* in mathematical terms		11
To see why *this* is needed		12
Such tools could determine the effects of specific policies		19
To overcome *these difficulties*		20
This is a fruitful and powerful approach		26
To put *this principle* to the test		28

UNIT 2 Language of Science

IV Language enhancement

Task 6 Locate the phrases in the text and complete the table below by explaining the meaning of each italicized word in your own words. Pay attention to the writer's choice of the adjective or adverb for emphasis. The first one has been done for you.

Phrase	Meaning	Paragraph
hopelessly entangled	in a hopeless manner, desperately	2
reliably distinguish		3
desperately need		4
sensible conclusion		5
flimsy correlation		7
firm causation		7
legitimately comment		17
incredibly challenging		19
highly correlated		20
patently false		21
quantitatively compute		24

Task 7 Locate the words in the text. Try to work out their meanings in academic context, and identify their word class. The first one has been done for you.

Word	Meaning in academic context	Word class	Paragraph
algorithm	a series of mathematical steps, especially in a computer program, which will give you the answer to a particular kind of problem or question	noun	1
underpin			3
mantra			5
correlation			5
causation			5

(Continued)

Word	Meaning in academic context	Word class	Paragraph
bedrock			7
algebra			9
equation			9
agnostic			9
operation			11
operator			11
variable			11
replication			16
skew			17
subject			17
constant			19
streamline			25
mine			25
repurpose			25
consistency			27
proactive			28
disentangle			30
parse			30

Task 8 Locate the phrases in the text and try to work out their meanings in context. Think about how the writer uses these phrases below and the effect the writer's choice of language has on the reader. The first one has been done for you.

Phrase	Meaning	Paragraph
train on	to point or aim something at something	1
fly in the face of		1
game changer		14
causal inference		15

(Continued)

Phrase	Meaning	Paragraph
put... on a... footing		16
a panoply of		19
home in on		19
control for		19
hold on to		20
gain ground		27
tally with		28
silver bullet		30

V Reading skills: Identifying the logical order

Task 9 Put the sentences in the two tables below in a logical order to form new paragraphs. Underline the cohesive markers and annotate each paragraph with a flow chart that demonstrates the logical order.

Table 1

Sentence	Number
It said that people who presented with pneumonia were more likely to survive if they also had asthma.	
Yet the data gathered from multiple hospitals was indisputable: If you had asthma, your chances were better.	
In the mid-1990s, an algorithm trained on hospital admission data made a surprising prediction.	
This flew in the face of all medical knowledge, which said that asthmatic patients were at increased risk from the disease.	
What was going on?	
Annotation:	

Table 2

Sentence	Number
This would involve randomly assigning beachgoers into two subgroups of equal size.	
Both would then be let loose in shark-infested waters, and the number of shark attacks on each group compared.	
If we wanted to establish the true relationship between ice cream eating and shark attacks, the scientific best practice would be to carry out a randomized controlled trial.	
One group would be given ice creams and the other wouldn't.	
To see why this is needed, let's head back to the seaside.	
Annotation:	

 **Text B**

Welcome to the Fuzzy-Verse

Eddy Keming Chen

1　What links a heap of sand, the edge of a cloud and actor Patrick Stewart's baldness? If you are only vaguely grasping what I am getting at, you are on the right track: They are all examples of imprecision in our description of the world. How many grains of sand can you take away from the heap and still call it a heap? Where exactly does the cloud end and the sky begin? How many hairs is Patrick Stewart allowed to have, and of what length, before he is classed as not bald? It is hard—perhaps impossible—to tell.

2　Such vague concepts, with their messy boundaries and borderline cases, are all around us. Until now, we have tended to assume they represent imperfections in our state of knowledge, our ways of communication or our modes of description. At some

UNIT 2 Language of Science

level, we think, the world must be precisely defined. Underpinning its workings, in the end, are the laws of physics, which are expressed using cast-iron mathematical equations that admit no vagueness.

3   I'm not so sure that's the case. I think I have uncovered a fundamental physical law that is itself vague. The implications could be far reaching, potentially casting doubt on the ability of conventional mathematics to provide us with a full description of the universe—but also perhaps opening entirely new avenues to even better physical theories.

4   Philosophers like me have spent a lot of time thinking about vague terms such as "bald" and "heap". The heap question is known as the sorites paradox, and it was noted as early as the 4th century BC. If a million grains make a heap, then a million minus one grains also make a heap, as do a million minus two grains and so on. Follow that logic, and eventually a single grain also makes a heap. That is absurd. So should we accept that there is a sharp boundary, some number of grains, below which grains don't make a heap? That is hard to swallow, too.

5   Vagueness is pervasive in natural language, and yet it resists logical analysis. The principle of bivalence that is central to classical logic—every statement is either true or false—seems to fail for vague terms. Imagine Tom, who is a borderline case of "bald". It isn't true that Tom is bald. It isn't false that Tom is bald. Classical bivalent logic is at risk.

6   Philosophical reflections have identified three types of vagueness. First, there is semantic vagueness. This is just a feature of how we communicate. Perhaps some of the words we use really are so vague that they leave some statements in limbo, neither clearly true nor clearly false.

7   Second, it may be due to our ignorance of some facts. Even though it may not be clear how to draw a sharp boundary between bald and non-bald, or between heap and non-heap, there may be an objective cut-off that we aren't aware of. This we call epistemic vagueness, and it neatly preserves bivalent logic because there is a true or false answer to any statement, even if we don't know which it is.

8   Third, vagueness may be due to some genuine indeterminacy in the universe. This is called ontic vagueness. There are some objects we define using natural language, such as a cloud, or Mount Everest, that simply don't have exact boundaries in space or time.

9   While we can continue to debate what type of vagueness is at play in any one situation, one thing that unites most philosophers is that all of this has little to do with fundamental laws of nature. Vagueness may also appear in some high-level sciences, such as biology, where terms such as "cell" "organism" and "life" are imprecisely

defined—a virus of the sort that is exercising us right now seems to be a classic borderline case of a living organism, as a bundle of genetic material that can only replicate inside the cells of another organism. But that vagueness should disappear when we drill down to more fundamental levels of explanation.

10   Fundamental laws of nature are written in the exact, non-messy language of mathematics. Mathematics, as we currently conceive it, is built around set theory, and a mathematical set is the very definition of being not vague. Something is either a member of a set—the set of all odd numbers, say, or all numbers divisible by 11—or it isn't. Sets are rigidly defined via a notion of equality: If two sets have the same members, they are the same set. Similarly, any mathematical function, topological space or geometrical shape built from sets is precisely defined. It is hard to see how the fundamental laws of physics could be completely and faithfully expressed in these terms if they admitted any vagueness.

On the Margins

11   Take Isaac Newton's universal law of gravitation, for instance, or his second law of motion, force=mass × acceleration (F=ma). Physical laws such as these are arbitrary, in the sense that they are set by nature. From all the different ways the universe could be, these laws pick out a small subset of physically possible versions. They admit no borderline cases: The behaviour of objects within this reality will adhere to these equations exactly, no ifs, no buts.

12   These laws also have a quality that will become important later on: traceability. Our universe is sensitive to changes in the laws. Any shift in the gravitational constant, G, for example, will be felt by massive objects and will change, however slightly or significantly, the motion of planets around stars, the formation of galaxies, the distribution of matter in the cosmos or how a falling vase shatters when it hits the ground. G's exact value leaves a trace on the world. Similarly, if we change F=ma to $F=ma^{1.001}$, it would produce observable physical changes: For a given force acting on a given mass, the resulting acceleration would be less.

13   The same arguments hold with all other fundamental equations of physics, for example Erwin Schrodinger's equation that defines the evolution of a quantum system, or Albert Einstein's field equations of general relativity that determine the development of the universe at large.

14   Did I say all? I meant not quite all. There seems to be one essential element of fundamental physics that has every right to be considered a law, but doesn't fit into this pattern.

15 Its origin lies in the puzzling observation that while the fundamental equations of physics are all time-symmetric, meaning they work equally well backwards as forwards, the world around us is distinctly time-asymmetric and irreversible. An arrow of time exists, a fact often encapsulated in the second law of thermodynamics, which puts limits on the sort of processes that can occur in reality. Ice cubes melt when placed in a drink to cool it, for example, but don't spontaneously form in it.

16 Explaining why leads to an influential proposal known as the Past Hypothesis. It says that the universe had a very special starting condition: It was initially in a state of low entropy, one with a high degree of order. This is about as fundamental a law about how the universe works as we have—and yet it is screamingly vague. In its weakest version, it simply says that the initial state of the universe has low entropy. How low is low?

17 I call this potential vagueness in a fundamental physical law "nomic vagueness". It seems distinct from the three other types of vagueness, and may be more basic. But let's take a closer look at what it consists of in the case of the Past Hypothesis.

18 First, its vagueness can be specified in a more precise way. We can characterize the initial state of the universe in terms of macroscopic variables such as temperature, volume, pressure and entropy, in accordance with astrophysical data. However, in classical statistical mechanics, this microstate corresponds to any number of microstates of individual particles with different positions and velocities. Many different microstates look essentially the same to us as we measure the microstate. Which microstates correspond to which microstate is only vaguely defined. There are always going to be borderline cases where a particular configuration of particles might amount to an initial state of that particular temperature, say—or might not.

19 But what if we just stipulate the exact boundaries of the microstate by saying the initial state of the universe corresponds to this set of possible microstates and no others? Let us call this the Strong Past Hypothesis. It means that any vagueness about the universe's initial state is due to our inexact knowledge of its microstate. This is then similar to the epistemic vagueness we discussed earlier. So, nothing to see here?

Untraceable Laws

20 The problem is that this Strong Past Hypothesis is arbitrary, and not just in the way other laws or constants are arbitrary. It is untraceably arbitrary: Whereas changing the value of the gravitational constant makes a difference to what the universe is like, there are infinitely many ways of wiggling the boundary of the initial microstate that make no difference to what the universe is like or even the probabilities of events within it.

21   This leaves us on the horns of a dilemma: We either embrace nomic vagueness or nomic untraceability. That is to some extent a matter of taste, but I suggest we should avoid untraceability. Observations of the universe often can uncover the nature of traceable laws. By contrast, untraceable laws can't be pinned down by facts. We can't do science to determine what they are; there is a gap between untraceable laws and the world.

22   A resolution to this dilemma might still come from within physics, and from a rather surprising quarter-quantum theory.

23   At first glance, this would seem to be the last place to look to banish vagueness from physical laws. Quantum objects such as particles are described by "wave functions" that have no definite locations in space or other exactly defined properties. Besides reality thus apparently becoming riddled with ontic vagueness, the very process of measurement that resolves this vagueness, "collapsing" quantum wave functions into exact states, is itself painfully vaguely defined. In the words of physicist John Stewart Bell: "What exactly qualifies some physical systems to play the role of 'measurer'? Was the wave function of the world waiting to jump for thousands of millions of years until a single-celled living creature appeared? Or did it have to wait a little longer, for some better qualified system... with a Ph.D.?"

24   Vagueness is indeed a feature of orthodox quantum theory—but other competing interpretations are also available. In the many-worlds interpretation, when we probe a quantum system, the universe divides according to the possibilities we might see. There is no vagueness at the fundamental level in this depiction: The fundamental stuff is always exactly defined, and the dynamical laws are exactly specified. Meanwhile, in Bohmian mechanics, also known as pilot-wave theory, a single universe evolves deterministically at all times in accordance with exact mathematical equation. And in "spontaneous collapse" theories, wave-function collapse is just a random and spontaneous feature of the universe's dynamical laws, banishing any vague or mystical special role for the measurer.

25   How might this help with the Past Hypothesis? The details are complex, but it amounts to the fact that, unlike classical mechanics, quantum mechanics allows us to connect the initial microstate and microstate of the universe in an exact, traceable way. Traditionally, the initial quantum state of the universe is described by a wave function, and the Past Hypothesis restricts the possible wave functions to a small subset compatible with a low-entropy macrostate. Work I have done shows that we can specify the initial state of the universe as something equivalent to a sum over all these possible wave functions.

Fundamentally Vague?

26   In pilot-wave theories and many-worlds theories, the form of the resulting "initial density matrix" will influence how things evolve subsequently; in spontaneous collapse theories, it will determine how collapses randomly happen. Changes to the initial density matrix will typically alter what the universe is like, just as is the case with other dynamical constants and laws. Thus quantum theory helps us to preserve both nomic exactness and traceability.

27   But there is no guarantee that such a solution is possible: We are far from achieving a quantum description of the beginning of the universe, and it may well be that a final theory of the nature of reality may not be fully quantum. If so, we again find ourselves on the horns of our dilemma, forced to admit nomic vagueness—and the consequences could be profound, not least for our ability to use mathematics to describe the universe. Any way of capturing a fundamental, yet vague, law such as the Past Hypothesis using traditional mathematics based on set theory will miss out something, or will impose too much sharpness somewhere.

28   This is perhaps an opportunity to think beyond classical mathematics for describing the universe. Other foundations besides set theory do exist for mathematics. Category theory, for example, focuses not on which mathematical objects are in which set, but on the abstract relationships between objects. Then there is homotopy type theory, which relaxes the notion of equality between objects central to set theory and defines objects in terms of paths between points in an abstract space. Either approach might provide a better language for capturing all physical laws, offering more flexibility in dealing with vagueness. Equally, it is possible that no mathematics can deal with it.

29   What about future laws of physics? That is a big unknown. But if nomic vagueness is possible, perhaps we don't have to restrict ourselves to formulating laws that can only be stated in precise mathematics. For example, the physicists Abhay Ashtekar and Brajesh Gupt have recently done some work on loop quantum gravity, one promising approach to unifying quantum theory with Einstein's theory of gravity, general relativity. Their proposal of an initial condition for the universe could be an instance of nomic vagueness, because of a vague boundary of the "Planck regime", the earliest epoch of the universe when the quantum effects of gravity dominated all other forces. It is one hint that a final theory of physics might not be entirely mathematically expressible.

30   Mathematics will still remain extremely useful. But if there is nomic vagueness, it may never completely capture the objective order of the universe. It may turn out that

vagueness runs far deeper than defining the number of grains of sand in a heap or of the hairs on a bald man's head. (*New Scientist*, September 5, 2020)

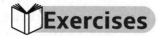

I Fast reading

Task 1 Tick (√) the statement that most closely reflects the writer's point of view.

(   ) A. The laws of nature that describe the universe are always exact.

(   ) B. Some fundamental laws are vague, and this phenomenon is called nomic vagueness, the existence of which raises interesting questions about the mathematical expressibility and metaphysical status of fundamental laws.

(   ) C. Nomic vagueness cannot be characterized as the existence of the borderline lawful world.

(   ) D. The dilemma between nomic vagueness and untraceable arbitrariness is dissolved in classical mechanics rather than in quantum mechanics.

II Annotating skills

Task 2 Identify which functions the following paragraphs of the text have, complete the table below using the annotations you have made, and find key information in relevant paragraphs as extra comment. The first one has been done for you.

◆ background information	◆ general problem	◆ solution
◆ exemplification	◆ cause	◆ explication
◆ implication	◆ evaluation	◆ viewpoint

UNIT **2** Language of Science

- definition
- comparison & contrast
- transition
- conclusion
- summary

Paragraph(s)	Function	Extra comment
1–2	general problem	problems found from experiences in our daily life
3		
4–5		
6–8		
9–10		
11–13		
14		
15–17		
18–19		
20–21		
22		

III Reading for specific information

Task 3   Read Text B carefully, but as fast as you can. Try to answer as many questions as you can without referring to the text.

1. In what way are the laws of physics expressed according to the text?

2. If the fundamental physical law is itself vague, what is the implication that we could make?

3. What is the technical term for the heap question?

4. What are the three types of vagueness identified through philosophical reflections?

5. Can you give some examples for semantic vagueness?

6. What is the status of set theory in mathematics?

7. What is the vital quality of fundamental physical laws like Isaac Newton's universal law of gravitation and the second law of motion?

8. What is the difference between the fundamental equations of physics and the world around us according to the text?

9. What is the fourth type of vagueness "coined" by the writer? What are the features of it?

10. What is the resolution to the dilemma put forward by the writer?

11. If we think beyond classical mathematics for describing the universe, what are the alternatives?

12. What is the writer's prediction of the future laws of physics?

Task 4 Read the text and try to find the text-referring words in the table. Note down the idea or word(s) that each one refers to. The first one has been done for you.

Text-referring word(s)	Refers to...	Paragraph
I'm not sure *that's* the case	It refers to the last sentence in Paragraph 2: Underpinning its workings, in the end, are the laws of physics, which are expressed using cast-iron mathematical equations that admit no vagueness	3
Physical laws such as *these* are arbitrary		11
The same arguments hold with all other fundamental equations of physics		13
Its origin lies in the puzzling observation		15

UNIT **2** Language of Science

(Continued)

Text-referring word(s)	Refers to...	Paragraph
This is about as fundamental a law about how the universe works as we have		16
It seems distinct from *the three other types* of vagueness		17
This leaves us on the horns of a dilemma		21

IV Language enhancement

Task 5 Locate the words in the text. Try to work out their meanings in academic context and identify their word class. The first one has been done for you.

Word	Meaning in academic context	Word class	Paragraph
class	be regarded as belonging to certain group of things	verb	1
boundary			2
mode			2
working			2
law			2
avenue			3
minus			4
swallow			4
classical			5
reflection			6
exercise			9
odd			10

(Continued)

Word	Meaning in academic context	Word class	Paragraph
motion			11
arbitrary			11
evolution			13
irreversible			15
configuration			18
resolution			22
banish			23
function			23
specify			24
relax			28
formulate			29

Task 6 Locate the phrases in the text and try to work out their meanings in context. Think about how the writer uses these phrases below and the effect the writer's choice of language has on the reader. The first one has been done for you.

Phrase	Meaning	Paragraph
on the right track	acting or thinking in a way that is likely to result in success	1
cast-iron		2
leave… in limbo		6
drill down		9
act on		12
at large		13
arrow of time		15
on the horns of a dilemma		21

(Continued)

Phrase	Meaning	Paragraph
pin down		21
the last place		23
be riddled with		23

V Reading skills: Definition and explanation

Task 7 Read the list of definitions or explanations in the table below and find the term in the text that matches each one. Try to identify the roles these terms play in the arguments. The first one has been done for you.

Term	Definition or explanation	Paragraph
heap question	If a million grains make a heap, then a million minus one grains also make a heap, as do a million minus two grains, and eventually a single grain also makes a heap.	4
	Every statement is either true or false.	
	Some of the words we use really are so vague that they leave some statements in limbo, neither clearly true nor clearly false.	
	Even though it may not be clear how to draw a sharp boundary between bald and non-bald, or between heap and non-heap, there may be an objective cut-off that we aren't aware of.	
	vagueness produced by some genuine indeterminacy in the universe, as we define objects by using natural language that don't have exact boundaries in space or time	
	working equally well backwards as forwards	
	The universe had a very special starting condition: It was initially in a state of low entropy, one with a high degree of order.	

(Continued)

Term	Definition or explanation	Paragraph
	Any vagueness about the universe's initial state is due to our inexact knowledge of its microstate.	
	the earliest epoch of the universe when the quantum effects of gravity dominated all other forces	

UNIT 3

Artificial Intelligence

COVID-19's AI Revolution

Sandy Ong

Introduction

① On an upper floor, something stirs in the semi-darkness of a closed shopping centre. It stops in front of a clothing store, bathing the window display in searing light. No alarm bells sound, no security guards rush forth. The Sunburst UV Bot, with its 1,000 watts' worth of UVC light capable of "tearing apart strands of virus DNA", comes here every night, as well as to a few other malls and hospitals in Singapore. It is doing something that human workers would have done before the COVID-19 pandemic: cleaning.

② Similar scenes are occurring across the world. In Texan hospitals, Moxi delivers medications, lab samples and supplies. P. Guard enforces lockdown curfews on Tunisian streets. James the telepresence bot helps residents at Belgian care homes stay connected. Other robots scrub supermarket floors, deliver meals to people in quarantine and even help walk the dog. Meanwhile, non-embodied artificial intelligences are assisting in everything from contact tracing and cracking the coronavirus's genetic code to the logistics and customer fulfilment of an increasingly online commercial world.

③ This trend towards automation and roboticisation isn't new—but COVID-19 is vastly accelerating it. "What this pandemic has done is to make people extremely aware of hygiene and the need to distance", says Richard Pak at Clemson University in South Carolina. "In these times, robots and automation definitely provide a safety benefit."

④ And perhaps also a huge problem. Unemployment has shot up as coronavirus has hit the global economy. What happens if we emerge from the COVID-19 recession to find that jobs have permanently gone—with no plan B to keep us gainfully employed?

⑤ Many cheer the promise of self-driving vehicles, virtual assistants and other labour-saving innovations. It is hard to argue with technologies that can give us a customised massage, recommend something good on Netflix or allow us to pay for groceries with the tap of a phone. During the COVID-19 pandemic, such technologies have helped reduce public health risks by enabling many people to work from home, safeguarding productivity while allowing businesses to stay afloat.

6   Even before the pandemic, however, many people were worried about the potential long-term jobs fallout of the trend towards automation. One analysis by consulting firm McKinsey & Company in 2017 suggested that automation could displace up to 800 million jobs worldwide by 2030. Back in 2013, Carl Frey and Michael Osborne at the University of Oxford rather piquantly used a machine-learning algorithm to assess how easily different jobs could be automated. The study concluded that machines will be able to do 47 percent of all U.S. jobs in the coming two decades—a figure that remains relatively constant today, says Frey. "In the U.K., the estimates are at 35 percent."

Getting Serious

7   Faced with employees under lockdown and the need for strict social distancing measures in the workplace, many companies have been putting a rocket under those trends, either by looking at greater automation for the first time or by accelerating and extending existing plans.

8   "There's so much room for automation now," says Derik Pridmore, CEO of Osaro, a company in San Francisco that develops AI systems for warehouse robots. "If companies were thinking about it before, they're now doing something. If they were doing something, they're now actually deploying it. Everyone is moving up a phase in their seriousness about automation." In March, a survey by auditing firm Ernst & Young of around 2,900 executives in 46 countries found that more than three-quarters were taking measures to either change or reevaluate the speed of their automation processes.

9   Concrete steps include the likes of Amazon, Walmart and other big retailers deploying more robots to haul and pack goods in their warehouses, and YouTube and Twitter using more machines for content moderation. Chatbot use has also swelled: In March, PayPal was using such software to handle a record 65 percent of its message-based customer enquiries. IBM reported seeing a 40 percent jump in demand from February to April for its Watson Assistant software that firms such as U.S. retailer Macy's and car manufacturer Chevrolet use to handle online calls.

10   Pridmore says his firm has seen a big pickup in interest from basically every region, in every application and sector since the pandemic hit. His clients include a grocery chain in Australia that found demand had doubled as more people began cooking at home, rather than eating out. Osaro helped automate the firm's order-fulfilment and shelf-restocking processes to cope with the increased demand.

11   Chris Duddridge, managing director at UiPath, whose AI platforms help automate call centres in the U.K., India and other countries, echoes this sentiment. "The

pandemic was indeed an accelerator for the adoption of automation," he says. Software robots have been instrumental in helping his firm's clients deal with the "huge backlogs and unprecedented volumes of requests" during the crisis, he says. Anxiety about automation seems to be increasing in lockstep. As part of a recent survey conducted by the Center for the Governance of Change at IE University in Segovia, Spain, almost 2,900 people from countries were asked whether their governments should limit automation by law in order to save jobs and prevent technological unemployment. In January, 42 percent of respondents in Spain and 27 percent in China—two countries that bore the initial brunt of the pandemic—said "yes". Three months later, as COVID-19 worsened, those figures jumped to 55 and 54 percent, respectively.

12   Part of that is generalised economic worry. "If you look historically, what you often see is that automation anxiety tends to be particularly prevalent during economic downturns," says Frey. "Losing one's job when there is an abundance of others is not that bad, but if you lose your job in an economic downturn, chances are that you're going to struggle to find another." Perhaps the most infamous example, highlighted by Frey in his 2019 book *The Technology Trap*, was the Luddites, who smashed stocking frames, and mechanized looms and other trappings of the first industrial revolution in the U.K. The unrest was especially bad after the Napoleonic wars ended in 1815, when Europe slumped into a depression, weavers saw their wages cut by a third and food prices skyrocketed because of new tariffs imposed on foreign grain.

13   Today, the sheer number of sectors affected is compounding such fears. Automation-related upheaval already posed a big threat to warehouse and factory workers, but many others in white collar jobs may find themselves out of work too. Those include financial analysts and radiographers whose jobs involve a lot of routine analysis of specific forms of data. Many of those jobs can now be performed just as competently, if not more so, by an AI. "This is one of the first times in history where a mix of blue-and-white-collar jobs are affected," says roboticist Ayanna Howard at the Georgia Institute of Technology in Atlanta.

14   Whoever is affected, the trend tends to be a one-way street. "When automation is here, it's here to stay," says futurist Ravin Jesuthasan. "In the economics of robotics, once you've made the upfront investment, whether it's in hard dollars or soft dollars of retraining the workforce and getting behaviour change from customers, it's much easier to perpetuate."

15   It isn't all doom and gloom, says Frey. "The only thing that is worse than automation is no automation." The world has been on a long-term path of technology doing more work for us for good reason, he says—it has enabled higher productivity,

lowered costs, greater scalability, safer environments, more flexible working and improved connectivity, to name just a few things. "If you look back over the past 200 years, there's no question that people are better off today, in large part because of automation," says Frey.

16   Others say we shouldn't overstate the scale or speed of this new transition, even as COVID-19 gives new reasons to drive it forward. Automation doesn't come cheap: Firms need to have the funds to install new machinery and software, as well as time to reconfigure workplaces and retrain workers to use them. "Automation only happens when the technology is ready to be implemented," says John Etchemendy at the Stanford Institute for Human-Centered Artificial Intelligence in California. "If the technology is not yet there, is not yet ready to take over the task, then the pandemic is not going to accelerate that."

17   "Our fear is often based on our science-fictional notion of robots replacing us," says roboticist Kate Darling at the Massachusetts Institute of Technology. To be convinced that we are "on the cusp of massive robot job-takeovers" would be to overestimate what robots and AI are capable of, she says. "COVID-19 may accelerate some investment, but we're looking at a longer time period than most people think."

18   Many tasks are still too delicate or complex to be automated, such as assembling a smartphone, cleaning elevator buttons or delivering the post. Others, such as confirming a medical diagnosis, still require human insight and interpretation, even if AIs can do some of the legwork. Then there are undertakings that simply cannot do without the warmth of a human touch. Most of the world is a long way from accepting robot therapists or nurses, for example.

19   With this wave of innovation, as with previous ones, the jobs most ripe for automation are those that are repetitive and dull. Few people have ever begged for one more spreadsheet to fill or one more box to pack, after all. Here, technology can remove tedium and free up people to do more meaningful work. More often than not, they end up working in partnership with machines—algorithms can trawl through countless transactions or medical images and flag up suspicious ones for a person to review, for example.

Work Redefined

20   Economist James Bessen at Boston University in Massachusetts agrees with that assessment. What we are likely to see isn't fewer jobs overall, but different ones. "There's no evidence that AI will lead to massive unemployment, but there will be increased churn," he says. "Automation can actually lead to new jobs." Already, we are seeing an

increase in demand for the likes of drone operators, data scientists, cryptographers, digital marketing specialists, video tech support and virtual event organisers. In the future, says Howard, we are going to need robot mechanics and customer service officers capable of handling people "so they aren't mad at a robot anymore".

21 That will require new training. "Jobs will be redefined," says Howard. Many experts suggest a sure-fire way to cushion against the economic effects of automation in the post-coronavirus era: invest in education, and specifically re-education. "At the heart of it is ensuring that anyone can engage with upskilling and reskilling in bite-sized chunks," says Jesuthasan, "as opposed to this fixation on a three- or four-year degree where you're somehow expected to be relevant for 30 years after. I think the world has moved on very rapidly from that legacy model."

22 This needs workers to adopt an open mindset to learning, but governments and firms must step in and help too by offering subsidised adult education courses, retraining programmes and other types of learning to help people make the necessary transitions. All this should be part of any post-COVID-19 recovery scheme. "Otherwise, left purely to market forces, you're going to find lots and lots of people left behind," says Jesuthasan.

23 There are other challenges we will have to face as the trend towards automation accelerates. One major issue is that AI has a tendency to inherit and amplify biases that exist in the data used to train it—for example, against minority ethnicity or lower-income groups. Then there are questions about how to frame laws around the responsible use of machines with ever-increasing autonomy, and the possibility of a growing social divide between those who can afford technology and those who can't.

24 Finding solutions requires having the headspace to think these things through, and that is difficult in the middle of a global pandemic. "We're still in a very reactive mode," says Howard. "To think about what comes next requires you to pause, and right now we're not in that state of luxury to be able to pause."

25 Get things right, though, and we can embrace the opportunities afforded by new tech, rather than being hampered by fear. As the threat of COVID-19 persists, devices like the virus-killing Sunburst UV Bot may be redefining certain jobs, but they are also making it safer for us to get on with others. (*New Scientists*, October 10, 2020)

UNIT **3** Artificial Intelligence

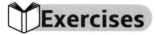

I Fast reading

Task 1 Think about the title of the text. How does COVID-19 relate to the AI revolution?

Task 2 Tick (√) the statement that most closely reflects the writer's point of view.

(   ) A. Unemployment has shot up as coronavirus has hit the global economy.

(   ) B. Many cheer the promise of self-driving vehicles, virtual assistants and other labor-saving innovations.

(   ) C. Many people were worried about the potential long-term jobs fallout of the trend towards automation.

(   ) D. Automation was already taking over jobs, but coronavirus pandemic is hugely accelerating the trend. Should we be worried? The answer is obviously no.

II Annotating skills

Task 3 Differentiate between main ideas and supporting sentences. Study the information in the following sentences, select three sentences which are main ideas, and match them with relevant sections in the text.

1. Meanwhile, non-embodied artificial intelligences are assisting in everything from contact tracing and cracking the coronavirus's genetic code to the logistics and customer fulfilment of an increasingly online commercial world.

2. This trend towards automation and roboticisation isn't new—but COVID-19 is vastly accelerating it.

3. Concrete steps include the likes of Amazon, Walmart and other big retailers deploying more robots to haul and pack goods in their warehouses, and YouTube and Twitter using more machines for content moderation.

4. The pandemic was indeed an accelerator for the adoption of automation, part of which is generalized economic worry.

5. According to scientists, jobs will be redefined.

6. There are other challenges we will have to face as the trend towards automation accelerates.

Section heading	Sentence
Introduction	
Getting Serious	
Work Redefined	

III Reading for specific information

Task 4 Read Text A carefully, but as fast as you can. Try to answer as many questions as you can without referring to the text.

1. What do Paragraphs 1 and 2 serve as?

2. Why do some scientists argue that COVID-19 is accelerating the trend towards automation and roboticisation?

3. How do people think of some labor-saving innovations like self-driving vehicles and virtual assistants?

4. As for the trend towards automation, what were people worried about even before the pandemic?

5. What did many companies do during the pandemic? Give some examples.

6. What example did Frey give in his 2019 book *The Technology Trap*?

7. Who would be affected mostly by automation?

8. According to Frey, what advantages does technology have?

9. What is our fear based on, according to roboticist Darling?

UNIT 3 Artificial Intelligence

10. What does Bessen think of AI?

11. What do experts suggest to deal with the trend of automation and roboticisation?

12. According to the writer, what is the major issue we have to face as the trend towards automation accelerates?

Task 5 In Text A, the opinions of a number of experts are mentioned. Read the opinions below. Then scan the text for information, matching each opinion to the relevant expert. The first one has been done for you.

| Chris Duddridge | Richard Pak | Derik Pridmore | Carl Frey |
| Ayanna Howard | John Etchemendy | Ravin Jesuthasan | |

1. The study concluded that machines will be able to do 47 percent of all U.S. jobs in the coming two decades—a figure that remains relatively constant today.   _Carl Frey_

2. What this pandemic has done is to make people extremely aware of hygiene and the need to distance. In these times, robots and automation definitely provide a safety benefit. _____

3. If companies were thinking about it before, they're now doing something. If they were doing something, they're now actually deploying it. Everyone is moving up a phase in their seriousness about automation. _____

4. The pandemic was indeed an accelerator for the adoption of automation. _____

5. Losing one's job when there is an abundance of others is not that bad, but if you lose your job in an economic downturn, chances are that you're going to struggle to find another. _____

6. This is one of the first times in history where a mix of blue-and-white-collar jobs are affected. _____

7. In the economics of robotics, once you've made the upfront investment, whether it's in hard dollars or soft dollars of retraining the workforce and getting behaviour change from customers, it's much easier to perpetuate. _____

8. If the technology is not yet there, is not yet ready to take over the task, then the pandemic is not going to accelerate that. _____

9. We are going to need robot mechanics and customer service officers capable of handling people "so they aren't mad at a robot anymore". _____

10. At the heart of it is ensuring that anyone can engage with upskilling and reskilling in bite-sized chunks, as opposed to this fixation on a three or four-year degree where you're somehow expected to be relevant for 30 years after. I think the world has moved on very rapidly from that legacy model. _____

11. We're still in a very reactive mode. To think about what comes next requires you to pause, and right now we're not in that state of luxury to be able to pause. _____

IV Language enhancement

Task 6 Study the words or phrases in the table below and identify them in the text. Try to work out their meanings by using the context in which you find them without using a dictionary. The first one has been done for you.

Word or phrase	Possible meaning	Paragraph
searing	very intense	1
in quarantine		2
shot up		3
fallout		6
brunt		11
compound		13
perpetuate		14
trawl		19
cushion		21
subsidize		22

V Reading skills: Making notes

Task 7 Complete the following notes on new jobs and challenges from the section of "Work Redefined", using as few words as possible.

New jobs of automation:

1. _____
2. _____
3. _____
4. _____
5. _____

Challenges we are faced with:

1. _____
2. _____
3. _____
4. _____
5. _____

Hunting for New Drugs with AI

David H. Freedman

1 There are three reasons that promising drugs wash out during pharmaceutical development, and one of them is cytochrome P450. A set of enzymes mostly produced in the liver, CYP450, as it is commonly called, is involved in breaking down chemicals

and preventing them from building up to dangerous levels in the bloodstream. Many experimental drugs, it turns out, inhibit the production of CYP450—a vexing side effect that can render such a drug toxic in humans.

2　Drug companies have long relied on conventional tools to try to predict whether a drug candidate will inhibit CYP450 in patients, such as by conducting chemical analyses in test tubes, looking at CYP450 interactions with better-understood drugs that have chemical similarities, and running tests on mice. But their predictions are wrong about a third of the time. In those cases, CYP450-related toxicity may come to light only during human trials, resulting in millions of dollars and years of effort going to waste. This costly inaccuracy can, at times, feel like "the bane of our existence", says Saurabh Saha, senior vice president of research and development and translational medicine at Bristol-Myers Squibb.

3　Inefficiencies such as this one contribute to a larger problem: The $1-trillion global pharmaceutical industry has been in a drug development and productivity slide for at least two decades. Pharmaceutical companies are spending more and more—the 10 largest ones now pay nearly $80 billion a year—to come up with fewer and fewer successful drugs. Ten years ago every dollar invested in research and development saw a return of 10 cents; today it yields less than two cents. In part, that is because the drugs that are easiest to find and that safely and effectively treat common disorders have all been found; what is left is hunting for drugs that address problems with complex and elusive solutions and that would treat disorders affecting only tiny portions of the population—and thus could return far less in revenue.

4　Because finding new, successful drugs has become so much harder, the average cost of bringing one to market nearly doubled between 2003 and 2013 to $2.6 billion, according to the Tufts Center for the Study of Drug Development. These same challenges have increased the lab-to-market time line to 12 years, with 90 percent of drugs washing out in one of the phases of human trials.

5　It's no wonder, then, that the industry is enthusiastic about artificial-intelligence tools for drug development. These tools do not work by having expert-developed analytical techniques programmed into them; rather users feed them sample problems (a molecule) and solutions (how the molecule ultimately behaves as a drug) so that the software can develop its own computational approaches for producing those same solutions.

6　Most AI-based drug-discovery applications take the form of a technique called machine learning, including a subset of the approach called deep learning. Most machine-learning programs can work with small data sets that are organized and labeled, whereas deep-learning programs can work with raw, unstructured data and require much larger volumes. Thus, a machine-learning program might learn to recognize the different features of a cell after being shown tens of thousands of examples of photographs of cells in which the parts are already labeled. A deep-learning version can figure out those parts on its own from unlabeled cell images, but it might need to look at a million of them to do it.

7   Many scientists in the field think that AI will ultimately improve drug development in several ways: by identifying more promising drug candidates; by raising the "hit rate", or the percentage of candidates that make it through clinical trials and gain regulatory approval; and by speeding up the overall process. A machine-learning program recently deployed by Bristol-Myers Squibb, for instance, was trained to find patterns in data that correlate with CYP450 inhibition. Saha says the program boosted the accuracy of its CYP450 predictions to 95 percent, a sixfold reduction in the failure rate compared with conventional methods. These results help researchers quickly screen out potentially toxic drugs and focus instead on candidates that have a stronger shot at making it all the way through multiple human trials to U.S. Food and Drug Administration approval. "Where AI can make a huge difference is having drugs that fail early on, before we make all that investment in them," says Vipin Go-pal, chief data and analytics officer at Eli Lilly.

8   Resources are now piling into the field. AI-based drug-discovery start-ups raised more than $1 billion in funding in 2018, and as of last September, they were on track to raise $1.5 billion in 2019. Every one of the major pharmaceutical companies has announced a partnership with at least one such firm. Only a few AI-discovered drugs are actually in the human-testing pipeline, however, and none has begun phase 3 human trials, the gold-standard test for experimental drugs. Saha concedes that it will be several years before he can say for sure whether the company's hit rates will go up as a result of the AI prediction rate of CYP450 inhibition. For all the hype in the industry, it is far from certain that early results will translate to more and better drugs.

Sifting Through Millions of Molecules

9   Emerging AI programs are not exactly a revolutionary up-date in the drug industry, which has for some time been building sophisticated analytical solutions that aid with drug development. The rise of powerful statistical and biophysical modeling programs well over a decade ago as part of the growth of the field of bioinformatics—the quest to use computational tools to derive biological insights from large amounts

of data—led to tools that can predict the properties of molecules. But these programs have been limited by scientists' incomplete understanding of how molecules interact: They cannot tell conventional software how to find insights in data when they do not know what elements of the data are most important and how they relate to one another. Imbued with the ability to derive their own insights into which data elements matter, newer AI programs can extract better predictions for a wider range of variables.

10 AI tools tackle different aspects of drug discovery in several ways. Some AI companies, for example, are focusing on the problem of designing a drug that can safely and effectively work on a known target—usually a specific, well-studied protein that is associated with a disease. The goal is typically to come up with a molecule that can chemically bind to the target protein and modify it so that it no longer contributes to the disease or its symptoms. Cyclica, a Canadian firm, puts its software to work on matching the biophysical structures and biochemical properties of millions of molecules to the structures and properties of some 150,000 proteins to uncover molecules likely to bind to target proteins, as well as those to avoid.

11 But molecules that are good candidates as drugs still have to jump through other hoops. Those include making it through the gut into the blood-stream without being immediately broken down by the liver or metabolic processes; working in a particular organ such as the kidney without disrupting other organs; avoiding binding to and incapacitating any of the thousands of other proteins in the human body that are important to health; and breaking down and leaving the body before drug levels become potentially dangerous. Cyclica's AI software takes all those requirements into consideration. "A molecule that can interact with a protein target can usually interact with upward of 300 proteins," Cyclica's CEO Naheed Kurji says. "If you're designing a molecule, it behooves you to consider the other 299 interactions that could have disastrous effects in humans."

12 There is growing recognition among biomedical researchers that complex diseases such as cancer and Alzheimer's involve hundreds of proteins, and hitting just one of them is not likely to be disruptive enough. Cyclica is attempting to find individual compounds that can interact with dozens of target proteins yet avoid interacting with hundreds of other proteins, Kurji explains. Currently under development, he adds, is the incorporation of a wealth of anonymized global genetic data about variations in proteins, so that the software can specify which patients the candidate drugs would work best on. Kurji claims that together these features will eventually be able to shave five years off the typical seven-year-long time frame for bringing a candidate drug from initial identification to human trials.

13   Merck and Bayer are among the big pharma companies that have announced partnerships with Cyclica. As is the case with most AI-pharma partnerships, the companies are not releasing much insight into exactly what AI-generated drug candidates may be coming out of the collaborations. But Cyclica has shared some details of its successes in identifying a key target protein linked to already FDA-approved drugs for systemic scleroderma, an autoimmune disease of the skin and other organs, as well as one linked to the Ebola virus. Each drug is already FDA-approved for the treatment of other disorders—HIV and depression, respectively—which means they both could be quickly "repurposed" for the new applications if the research continues to pan out.

14   Sometimes researchers identify a target protein that might play a critical role in disease but find that—as is true of about 90 percent of the proteins in the human body—not much is known about its structure and properties. With little data to go on, most machine- and deep-learning programs will not be able to figure out how to "drug" the protein—that is, come up with compounds that will bind to it and meet the other criteria for safety and efficacy. A handful of AI companies are focusing on these kinds of "small data" problems, including Exscientia, which uses its software to hunt down molecules that might work with a target protein. It can produce useful insights with as few as 10 pieces of data about a protein, says the company's CEO, Andrew Hopkins, a professor of medicinal informatics at the University of Dundee in Scotland.

15   Exscientia's algorithms compare the limited information available about a target protein against a database of about a billion protein interactions. This step narrows down the list of possible compounds that might work and specifies what additional data would help further refine the focus. Such data might come from looking at tissue samples to learn more about how the protein behaves in the body, for example. The resulting new data are then fed into the software, which pares the list again and suggests another round of needed data. This process is repeated until the software is ready to generate a manageable list of compounds that are favorable drug candidates for the target.

16   Hopkins claims that Exscientia's process can cut the time spent in discovery from 4.5 years to as little as one year, reduces discovery costs by 80 percent and results in one-fifth the number of synthesized compounds as is normally needed to produce a single winning drug. Exscientia is partnering with biotech giant Celgene in an effort to find new potential drugs for three targets.

17   Meanwhile an Exscientia partnership with GlaxoSmithKline has led to what the companies say is a promising molecule targeting a novel pathway to treat chronic obstructive pulmonary disease. But as with any AI company addressing drug

development, Exscientia simply has not been in the game long enough to have generated enough new candidates that could have made it through to late-stage trials—a process that typically takes five to eight years. Hopkins claims one of the candidates Exscientia has identified may reach human trials as early as this year. "At the end of the day we'll be judged on the drugs we deliver," he says.

The Need for New Targets

18 Finding a molecule to hit a new target is not the only major challenge in drug discovery. There is also the need to identify targets in the first place. To spot proteins that might have roles in diseases, biopharma company Berg applies AI to sift through information derived from human tissue samples. This approach aims to solve two problems that hang over most research into drug targets, according to Berg's CEO Niven R. Narain: The efforts tend to be based on a researcher's theory or hunch, which can bias the results and overly restrict the pool of candidates, and they often turn up targets that are correlated to the disease but do not ultimately prove causative, which means drugging them will not help.

19 Berg's approach involves plugging in every piece of data that can be wrung out of a patient's tissue samples, organ fluids and bloodwork. These extracted data include genomics, proteomics, metabolomics, lipidomics, and more—an unusually broad range to consider in a hunt for targets. Samples are taken from people with and without a particular disease and at different stages of disease progression. Living cells from the samples are exposed in the laboratory to various compounds and conditions, such as low levels of oxygen or high levels of glucose. This method produces data on corresponding changes ranging from a cell's ability to produce energy to the rigidity of its membrane.

20 All the data are then run through a set of deep-learning programs that search for any differences between nondisease and disease states, with an eye to eventually focusing on proteins whose presence seems to have an impact on the disease. In some cases, those proteins become candidates as targets, at which point Berg's software can start searching for compounds to drug those targets. What is more, because the software can discern when the target seems to cause disease in only a subset of patients, it can look for distinguishing characteristics of those patients, such as certain genes. That paves the way for a precision-medicine approach, meaning patients can be tested before they take the drug to determine whether it is likely to be effective for them.

21 The most exciting drug to come out of Berg's work—and perhaps the most exciting to emerge from any drug-discovery-related AI effort to date—is a cancer drug called

BPM31510. It recently completed a phase 2 trial for patients with advanced pancreatic cancer, which is extremely aggressive and difficult to treat. Phase 1 trials often do not indicate much about a drug's potential except whether it is dangerously toxic at a given dose, but BPM31510's phase 1 trial against other cancers provided some verification of the ability of Berg's software to predict the roughly 20 percent of patients who were likely to respond to it, as well as those who were more likely to experience adverse reactions.

22   Additionally, tissue-sample analysis from the trial led Berg's software to predict, counterintuitively, that the drug would work best against more aggressive cancers because it attacks mechanisms that play a larger role in those cancers. Should the drug gain approval, Berg might do a postmarket analysis of perhaps one out of 100 patients taking it, "so that we can keep improving how it's used," Narain says.

23   Berg is partnering with pharma giant AstraZeneca to seek targets for Parkinson's and other neurological diseases and with Sanofi Pasteur to pursue improved flu vaccines. It is also working with the U.S. Department of Veterans Affairs and the Cleveland Clinic on targets for prostate cancer. The software has already identified mechanisms for diagnostic tests that could differentiate prostate cancer from benignly enlarged prostates, which currently is often difficult to do without surgery.

Getting Beyond the Hype

24   Big pharma's interest in injecting these kinds of AI efforts into drug discovery can be gauged by the fact that at least 20 separate partnerships have been reported between the major companies and AI-drug-discovery tech companies. Pfizer, GlaxoSmithKline and Novartis are among the pharma companies said to have also built substantial AI expertise in-house, and it is likely that others are in the process of doing the same.

25   Although research executives at these companies have expressed enthusiasm for some of the early results, they are quick to admit that AI is no sure thing for the bottom line given how few new AI-aided candidates have made it to the animal-testing stage of drug development, let alone to human trials. The jury is out on whether AI will successfully make drug discovery more efficient, says Sara Kenkare-Mitra, senior vice president of development sciences at Roche subsidiary Genentech, and even if it does, "we can't yet say whether it will be an incremental improvement or an exponential leap." If many of the drugs that result from AI efforts make it well into human testing, this question will still not be answered fully unless the drugs progress all the way through to FDA approval.

26   Bristol-Myers Squibb's Saha suggests that AI-aided drugs' rate of entry into the

market is likely to remain low for some time. That rate could pick up dramatically, however, if the processes for testing and approval were streamlined to take into account the ability of machine- and deep-learning systems to more accurately predict which drugs are highly likely to be safe and effective and which patients they are best suited for. "When regulatory agencies see the same value we see in AI, the flood gates could open," he says. "In some cases, we might be allowed to pass over animal models and go straight to human testing once we show these drugs can hit their targets with no toxicity." But those changes are probably many years away, he admits. He adds that it is wrong to imply that AI replaces scientists and conventional research—whereas AI supports and amplifies human efforts, it still depends on humans to generate novel biological insights, set research directions and priorities, guide and validate results, and produce needed data.

27 The breathless hype around AI-based drug discovery might actually be damaging, Berg's Narain says, because overpromising could lead to disappointment and backlash. "These are early days, and we need to be sober about the fact that these are tools that can help—they're not solutions yet," he says. Cyclica's Kurji points the finger at AI companies that make what he says are exaggerated marketing claims, such as having reduced the many years and billions of dollars it takes to develop a drug to a few weeks and a few hundred thousand dollars. "It's simply not true," he says. "And it's irresponsible and destructive to say so."

28 But if hype hurts, Kurji insists he also knows what will give the AI-drug-discovery industry a big boost: more high-quality information to feed the various programs. "We rely on three things: data, data and more data," he says. That sentiment is echoed by Enoch Huang, vice president of medicinal sciences at Pfizer, who says that having the right algorithm isn't the most important factor.

29 The need to feed AI software with large volumes of relevant data is actually starting to change science, as researchers run more experiments specifically with the production of AI-relevant data in mind. Genentech's Kenkare-Mitra notes that this has already happened in immunotherapy drug research. "There aren't always enough data from the clinic to use with machine learning," she says. "But we can [often] generate that data in vitro and feed them to the system."

30 That kind of approach could lead to a virtuous cycle in drug discovery in which AI helps elucidate areas where researchers need to look for targets and drugs. Moreover, the resulting research provides larger, more relevant data sets that allow the software to point to even more fertile research avenues. "It's not so much AI we believe in," Kenkare-Mitra says, "as a human-AI partnership." (*Scientific American*, February 2020)

UNIT **3** Artificial Intelligence

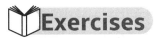

I Fast reading

Task 1 Tick (√) the statement that most closely reflects the writer's point of view.

(   ) A. Many drug companies are piling resources into drug discovery with AI tools.

(   ) B. The pharmaceutic industry is in a drug-discovery slump, and many scientists believe AI tools will replace scientists and conventional research.

(   ) C. Only a few AI-discovered drugs are actually in the human-testing pipeline, however, none has begun phase 3 human trials.

(   ) D. The pharmaceutic industry is in a drug-discovery slide. However, scientists think that AI tools will help.

II Annotating skills

Task 2 In Text B, the writer has made full use of the "problem-solution" pattern. Read the text carefully and complete the table below using the annotations you have made.

Paragraph(s)	Annotation: Problem and solution
1–4	**Problem:** Promising drugs 1) _____ during pharmaceutical development. For example, 2) _____, mostly produced in the liver, is involved in 3) _____ them from building up to dangerous levels in the bloodstream.
5–8	**Solution:** Many scientists think that 4) _____ will 5) _____ in several ways: 6) _____, 7) _____ and 8) _____. For instance, 9) _____ was trained to 10) _____ that 11) _____ with CYP450.

67

(Continued)

Paragraph(s)	Annotation: Problem and solution
9	**New problem:** AI programs have been limited by 12) _____: 13) _____ and 14) _____.
9–17	**Solution:** 15) _____, newer AI programs can 16) _____. For example, some AI companies are focusing on 17) _____. Cyclica 18) _____ to work on matching 19) _____ and 20) _____ to the structures and properties 21) _____. Exscientia is focusing on figuring out how to 22) _____, using its software to 23) _____. Exscientia's algorithms 24) _____ which 25) _____ and 26) _____. Its process can 27) _____, 28) _____ and 29) _____.
18	**New problem:** Another challenge is to 30) _____ before hitting a target.
18–23	**Solution:** Berg applies AI to 31) _____. Berg's approach 32) _____. This method produces 33) _____. All the data are run through 34) _____, with an eye to focusing on 35) _____.

III Reading for specific information

Task 3 Read Text B carefully, but as fast as you can. Try to answer as many questions as you can without referring to the text.

1. Why is the pharmaceutic industry in a drug-discovery slide according to the text?

2. What is CYP450? What roles does it play?

3. What do scientists do to deal with the slide?

4. What methods do scientists employ to develop new drugs with AI?

5. According to the experts, how will AI help to develop new drugs?

6. What limitations did bioinformatics have a decade ago?

UNIT 3　Artificial Intelligence

7. How can newer AI do to handle these limitations?

8. What has Cyclica done to develop new drugs with AI?

9. What difficulty have AI tools met with when hitting a target protein?

10. What does Exscientia do to identify a target protein?

11. In addition to hitting a target protein, what problem should be solved in the first place?

12. What does Berg do to identify targets with AI?

13. What does Sara Kenkare-Mitra say about AI in drug development?

14. What does Narain say about AI-based drug discovery?

15. What does Kurji think of AI companies' hype?

IV Language enhancement

Task 4 Study the words or phrases in the table below and identify them in the text. Try to work out their meanings by using the context in which you find them without using a dictionary. The first one has been done for you.

Word or phrase	Possible meaning	Paragraph
wash out	to eliminate through selection or competition	1
inhibit		1
vexing		1
elusive		3
boost		7
screen out		7
imbue with		9
hoop		11
shave... off		12

(Continued)

Word or phrase	Possible meaning	Paragraph
pan out		13
sift through		18
exponential		25
be sober about		27
elucidate		30

V Reading skills: Identifying reporting language

Task 5 Note the various ways, such as those in Paragraph 7, in which the writer reports other scientists' ideas and underline the reporting language.

1. Many scientists in the field think that AI will ultimately improve drug development in several ways.

2. Saha says the program boosted the accuracy of its CYP450 predictions to 95 percent, a sixfold reduction in the failure rate compared with conventional methods.

3. "Where AI can make a huge difference is having drugs that fail early on, before we make all that investment in them," says Vipin Go-pal, chief data and analytics officer at Eli Lilly.

Task 6 Look at the sentences above and decide whether each one is direct or indirect reporting. Tick (√) the appropriate column in the table below.

	1	2	3
Direct reporting			
Indirect reporting			

> Task 7   Read the sentences below and underline the reporting language.

1. Saha *concedes that* it will be several years before he can say for sure whether the company's hit rates will go up as a result of the AI prediction rate of CYP450 inhibition.

2. Cyclica is attempting to find individual compounds..., Kurji *explains*. Currently under development, he *adds*, is the incorporation of a wealth of anonymized global genetic data about variations in proteins.

3. Kurji *claims that* together these features will eventually be able to shave five years off the typical seven-year-long time frame for bringing a candidate drug from initial identification to human trials.

4. But Cyclica *has shared some details of* its successes in identifying a key target protein linked to already FDA-approved drugs for systemic scleroderma, an autoimmune disease of the skin and other organs, as well as one linked to the Ebola virus.

5. It can produce useful insights with as few as 10 pieces of data about a protein, *says* the company's CEO, Andrew Hopkins, a professor of medicinal informatics at the University of Dundee in Scotland.

UNIT 4

Computing Science

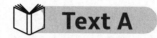

Number Crunch

Edd Gent

1 The modern world is drowning in data. In 1984, the global traffic of the fledgling Internet amounted to 15 gigabytes per month. By 2014, that had become the average traffic per user. In 2019, each of us burned through that much data in just over a week. The flood gates show no signs of closing, either. As billions of new users come online, and ever more devices become web-connected, the amount of data in the world is forecast to rise to 175 zettabytes (10^{21} bytes) by 2025—more than three times humanity's output to date.

2 Processing these oceans of data requires enormous infrastructure, extending beyond smartphones and personal computers to millions of energy-hungry data centres around the globe. That combined hum already uses 6 percent of the world's electricity, an energy bill predicted to double by 2030, raising concerns about the sustainability of our digital habits. For decades, technological improvements kept the rising waters at bay, allowing hardware to get smaller, faster and more energy efficient. But the silicon chips we rely on are starting to hit physical limits, threatening to leave us with an energy bill we can ill afford to pay.

3 A plethora of alternative technologies are vying to continue the upward march in processing power, but most are still languishing on the lab bench. That is why a growing number of researchers are calling for something more transformative: a complete rethink of the thermodynamics underpinning computing. If the idea gains traction, it could revolutionise how computers are designed, allow processors to grow more powerful without huge extra energy demands, and sate our growing appetite for data.

4 In 1961, IBM physicist Rolf Landauer set out to calculate the theoretical efficiency of a perfect computer—one that wasted none of its energy in combating resistance. He knew that such a device would still consume some energy. That is because, like all machines, computers are constantly fighting one of the most powerful forces in the universe: the second law of thermodynamics. This states that the disorder of any closed system—a measure known as entropy—will always increase. It is why eggs don't unscramble and marbles are easier to spill than clean up.

5   Landauer reasoned that corralling information is a rebellion against disorder and so represents a decrease in entropy that can only be bought with energy. He worked out that even the simplest computation possible—erasing a single bit—must incur a tiny thermodynamic debt, no smaller than 2.8×10^{-21} joules. Operating at this efficiency, Summit, the world's most mighty supercomputer, could be powered by a few milliwatts. In reality, it uses 13 megawatts, the approximate peak output of two offshore wind turbines.

6   Even this is astonishingly efficient compared with early computers. The Cray 1 supercomputer, unveiled in 1975, used roughly 1 percent of that power, but had less than a billionth of the computational muscle. The shift to where we are today was enabled by two remarkable trends working in tandem. The first was industry's ability to miniaturise transistors and double the number of them that could be squeezed on a computer chip roughly every two years, a trend referred to as Moore's law. The second was an observation from computer scientist Robert H. Dennard that the power consumption of individual transistors fell in proportion to their reduced size. This meant you could double a chip's computing power at the same time as its energy efficiency.

Breaking Moore's Law

7   However, these advances couldn't last forever. Roughly 15 years ago, silicon transistors started getting so small that further efficiency gains became physically impossible. Today, the number of transistors per chip continues to rise, but packing them closer together is getting increasingly complicated. This is because the extra heat given off causes chips to malfunction. "We are getting close to the limit of how efficient they can be." says Iris Bahar at Brown University in Rhode Island. For the first time in 50 years, Moore's law is beginning to falter.

8   At the same time, demand for ever smaller, ever more powerful computers is booming. Upgrading mobile data networks from 4G to 5G technology, which will make download speeds up to 100 times faster, is expected to see average monthly data use in North America balloon from 8.6 gigabytes per person in 2019 to 50 gigabytes in 2024. The so-called Internet of things spanned 9.5 billion devices in 2019 and is due to reach 28 billion by 2025. In 2017, Huawei researcher Anders Andrae predicted that the tsunami of data crunching resulting from all this would consume a fifth of the world's electricity by 2025. That figure understandably made headlines. His latest predictions are less apocalyptic, but still suggest that more than 10 percent of the world's electricity could be devoted to information processing by 2030. In terms of raw power, that would be more than what is currently used by the whole of the EU. Such growth is likely to

represent a significant future source of carbon emissions, and keeping data centres from overheating will require unsustainably vast quantities of cooling water.

9   Not everyone believes such a dramatic energy crunch is coming. "Andrae's models are pretty simplistic frankly," says Eric Masanet at Northwestern University in Illinois. He says they extrapolate from older studies of computing's energy use, an approach that has historically led to overestimates. In a recent study, Masanet and his colleagues found that the energy use of data centres only increased by 6 percent between 2010 and 2018 despite a 550 percent increase in their workload.

10   That was thanks to improvements in hardware as well as energy management, but Masanet thinks further efficiency gains will be required. "We need to start paying more attention to the potential for rapid growth in energy use and we need to start doing what we can to avert that," he says.

Turning down the Heat

11   That's precisely the motivation behind a host of alternative technologies hoping to exploit new materials or innovative means of manipulating data. But experts agree it will be many years before any provides sufficient improvement to head off the problems faced by computing.

12   A more radical approach may now be emerging. A growing number of researchers are revisiting Landauer's calculations and using new tools to dramatically expand our understanding of how thermodynamics and computing interact. For Jim Crutchfield at the University of California, Davis, computing's situation has parallels with the industrial revolution. In the 18th and 19th centuries, engines and pumps were built to convert heat into mechanical energy long before physicists formalised the principles of thermodynamics. When those principles were better understood, the gains in efficiency and power were astonishing. "We're in the information age and we're somewhat in the same conceptual situation," says Crutchfield. "The general claim is that if we understand these trade-offs, we're going to be able to design computers that are three or four orders of magnitude more energy-efficient."

13   The opportunity arises from what Landauer's work left out. For all its profundity, says David Wolpert at the Santa Fe Institute in New Mexico, it could only establish a maximum efficiency, not set out a roadmap to getting there. In part, that was due to the limited mathematical tools available at the time. They could only describe systems in equilibrium, where no energy enters or leaves, which is a massive oversimplification. "Computational systems are, if nothing else, extraordinarily non-equilibrium," says Wolpert. They are in constant flux, and information and energy flow in and out of

them all the time. In fact, almost nothing in the real world is in equilibrium, he says, something early computer pioneers were aware of but lacked the equations to describe.

14   There's another, equally important, property of equilibrium that the real world breaks. According to the laws of thermodynamics, an equilibrium system is in a state of perfect internal disorder—it has maximum entropy. But this is obviously not the case in everyday life, where the entropy of a system is constantly changing. Imagine pouring a jar of marbles down the stairs, for example. You know that all the marbles will eventually reach the bottom, but one or two might bounce backup some stairs on their way down. Averaged over the whole jar, this effect is insignificant, but on small distances and on short time scales, reversals of disorder are possible. The same dynamics play out at the nanoscale, a complexity that the traditional theory of thermodynamics couldn't predict or describe. This began to change in the late 1990s, when physicist Christopher Jarzynski and chemist Gavin Crooks developed equations that allow us to precisely predict when such entropy reversals happen and how much energy non-equilibrium processes really use. These findings were groundbreaking, says Wolpert.

15   In recent years, there has been a growing realization that this field could also help revolutionise computing, for example by charting the way to redesigning hardware as well as software to be more energy efficient using thermodynamic principles. "It's extraordinarily powerful," says Wolpert. "These tools they've developed can actually be used to go back and expand every single chapter in the computer science textbook." New equations built off the back of Crooks and Jarzynski's work can precisely calculate the energy required for a host of information processing tasks in much more realistic scenarios. Although Landauer's limit remains far off, that could open the door to enormous efficiency gains.

16   These advances are uncovering new layers of complexity, says Wolpert. Minimising the energy your circuit uses requires complex trade-offs between things like speed, accuracy and physical layout. Wolpert has developed equations that can precisely calculate the thermodynamic cost of different circuit designs. While the ideas are still at an early stage, they could allow us to build significantly more efficient circuits from the ground up. "This is taking the exact same devices and simply wiring them a different way," he says.

17   How far these ideas could take us is unclear, but proponents frequently point out that nature has already created a supercomputer that runs on a third of the energy your laptop uses—the human brain. This demonstrates that, at least in principle, new horizons are there to be unlocked. How nature achieves such efficiencies within the brain remains a mystery, but biology offers plenty of other examples of ultra-efficient

information processing. Cells rely on a cascade of reactions to process chemical signals from the outside world, operating only about 50 times above Landauer's limit. The process by which enzymes copy DNA is similarly efficient, leading Microsoft to start investigating it as a potential computing technology.

18 "The most exciting perspective is whether living systems compute in ways we are absolutely not aware of," says Massimiliano Esposito at the University of Luxembourg. From what we know so far, that seems likely. Today's computers march to an internal clock, churning through sequential tasks to produce consistent outputs. That predictability is hard-won. On the tiny scale of transistors, everything from overheating to manufacturing defects can throw computations off. Engineers deal with this by building in wide margins of error and plenty of redundancy, but that, in turn, increases the energy required per bit.

19 Wasting energy would be a major disadvantage for living systems, says Esposito, and most information processing in biology appears to maximise efficiency at the expense of other attributes like accuracy or speed. These are exactly the kinds of trade-offs non-equilibrium thermodynamics predicts.

20 As an example, most computers are governed by a single central processing unit that controls all other components. This centralization is powerful, but means billions of instructions need to be fired off every second with incredible accuracy, at significant energy cost. By contrast, nature gives every cell in the body the power to independently implement the instructions contained in DNA, allowing them to perform in unison without the need for a conductor. That means that a process like DNA copying is able to trade speed and reliability for far greater efficiency. If we want to mimic nature's extreme efficiency, we may have to borrow some of these ideas.

Computing 2.0

21 What such a dramatic paradigm shift would look like in computing is hard to imagine, admits Crutchfield, but it holds vast promise. Despite its rapid growth, the Internet of things is hamstrung by the need to power billions of small devices, often in locations that make them hard to recharge. In these circumstances, being able to mimic the slower—but ultra-low power—distributed computing seen in nature could be very attractive.

22 The hardware of the future is unlikely to stray far from today's chips and circuit boards, says Crutchfield, as that is the only approach we know how to scale. However, a hybrid approach combining traditional computing logic with components that

harness thermodynamic effects is a likely starting point. The cryogenically cooled superconducting circuits used in quantum computers hold promise too, says Crutchfield, as they can also operate under conditions where non-equilibrium physics dominates. He has recently teamed up with applied physicists to test some of the field's predictions on these circuits, and says they could conceivably be scaled up for more sophisticated computing.

23   Not everyone is sold. The most glaring problem is that most work so far has dealt with theoretical circuits processing just a few bits of information. On the scale of today's silicon chips, though, these thermodynamic benefits would pale into insignificance compared with the waste energy they produce. "I'm all in favour of theory, but sometimes it just ignores reality," says Eli Yablonovitch at the University of California, Berkeley.

24   Bridging the divide between theory and engineering will take a lot of work from both sides, says Stephanie Forrest of Arizona State University. For one thing, the new mathematical tools that work on the level of bits rapidly become intractable once you start scaling them up. She believes that significant mathematical shortcuts will be needed before real-world computers can start benefiting from these breakthroughs.

25   Crutchfield agrees. That is why his research programme for the next decade will be dominated by putting the new ideas to the test. All the same, he wouldn't be surprised to see significant progress before then. "Maybe in about five years, people are going to appreciate what a huge revolution this has been," he says. There are signs people are starting to appreciate it now. X, the so-called moonshot arm of tech giant Alphabet, recently hired Crooks to look into the potential applications of non-equilibrium thermodynamics. There are serious practical difficulties to putting these ideas to work, he says, but he doesn't see any fundamental barriers.

26   "It's not just a question of an incremental change in the energy dissipation of the things we've got now," says Crooks. "It would enable entirely new things." In a world awash with data, that could be just the lifeline we need. (*New Scientists*, March 14, 2020)

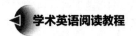

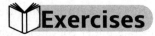

I Fast reading

Task 1 Tick (√) the statement that most closely reflects the writer's point of view.

(　) A. Processing lots of data requires enormous infrastructure, which raises our concerns about the sustainability of our digital habits.

(　) B. A great number of alternative technologies are competing to continue the upward march in processing power, but most are still failing in the lab.

(　) C. Since our appetite for data is becoming unsustainable, we urgently need to rethink computing.

(　) D. The number of transistors per chip continues to rise, but packing them closer together is getting increasingly complicated.

II Annotating skills

Task 2 Annotate the text in the margin. Look at the two examples of annotation for the extract from Paragraphs 6 and 9 of the text. Then highlight the parts of the text and identify their functions.

Annotations	Text extract from Paragraph 6
point of view _____ _____ _____	Even this is astonishingly efficient compared with early computers. The Cray 1 supercomputer, unveiled in 1975, used roughly 1 percent of that power, but had less than a billionth of the computational muscle. The shift to where we are today was enabled by two remarkable trends working in tandem. The first was industry's ability to miniaturise transistors and double the number of them that could be squeezed on a computer chip roughly every two years, a trend referred to as Moore's law. The second was an observation from

UNIT **4** Computing Science

(Continued)

Annotations	Text extract from Paragraph 6
_____	computer scientist Robert H. Dennard that the power consumption of individual transistors fell in proportion to their reduced size. This meant you could double a chip's computing power at the same time as its energy efficiency.

Annotations	Text extract from Paragraph 9
point of view _____ _____ _____	Not everyone believes such a dramatic energy crunch is coming. "Andrae's models are pretty simplistic frankly," says Eric Masanet at Northwestern University in Illinois. He says they extrapolate from older studies of computing's energy use, an approach that has historically led to overestimates. In a recent study, Masanet and his colleagues found that the energy use of data centres only increased by 6 percent between 2010 and 2018 despite a 550 percent increase in their workload.

Task 3 In Text A, the writer has made full use of the "problem-solution" pattern. Read the text carefully and complete the table below using the annotations you have made.

Paragraph(s)	Annotation: Problem and solution
3	**Problem:** A plethora of alternative technologies are vying to continue the upward march in 1) _____, but most are still 2) _____ on the lab bench. **Solution:** 3) _____.
7–8	**New problem:** The number of transistors per chip 4) _____, because the extra heat given off 5) _____, Moore's law 6) _____. At the same time, demand for 7) _____ _____. In 2017, Huawei researcher Anders Andrae predicted that 8) _____.
12	**Solution:** A more radical approach is to 9) _____. Jim Crutchfield believes 10) _____.

(Continued)

Paragraph(s)	Annotation: Problem and solution
13	**New problem:** Almost nothing in the real world is in equilibrium, David Wolpert says, something early computer pioneers were aware of 11) _____.
14–18	**Solution:** In the late 1990s, physicist Christopher Jarzynski and chemist Gavin Crooks 12) _____ that allow us to precisely predict 13) _____ and 14) _____. Wolpert has developed 15) _____ that can precisely 16) _____. But proponents point out that 17) _____ has already created a supercomputer that runs on a third of the energy your laptop uses—the human brain.
19	**New problem:** 18) _____ would be a major disadvantage for living systems, says Esposito, and most information processing in biology appears to maximise efficiency at the expense of other attributes like 19) _____.
21–22	**Solution:** Being able to mimic the slower—but ultra-low power— 20) _____ seen in nature could be very attractive. However, a hybrid approach combining 21) _____ that harness thermodynamic effects is a likely starting point. 22) _____ used in quantum computers hold promise too, says Crutchfield.
23	**New problem:** The most glaring problem is that most work so far has dealt with 23) _____ processing just a few bits of information.
24	**Solution:** According to Stephanie Forrest of Arizona State University, 24) _____ between theory and engineering will take a lot of work from both sides.

UNIT **4** Computing Science

III Reading for specific information

Task 4 Read Text A carefully, but as fast as you can. Try to answer as many questions as you can without referring to the text.

1. What consequence did our digital habits have?

2. Why are a growing number of researchers calling for a complete rethink of the thermodynamics underpinning computing?

3. What is entropy?

4. What did Landauer think about collecting information?

5. Why do scientists say that Moore's law is beginning to falter?

6. What did Andrae predict?

7. What did Masanet and his colleagues find?

8. Why are many researchers resisting Landauer's calculation?

9. What do scientists find about equilibrium according to the laws of thermodynamics?

10. What tools did Jarzynski and Crooks develop?

11. What has Wolpert developed?

12. What does Crutchfield think of the hardware of the future?

Task 5 Read the text and try to find the text-referring words in the table. Note down the idea or word(s) that each one refers to. The first one has been done for you.

Text-referring word(s)	Refers to...	Paragraph
By 2014, *that* had become the average traffic per user	15 gigabytes per month	1
That is why a growing number of researchers are calling for something more transformative		3

83

(Continued)

Text-referring word(s)	Refers to...	Paragraph
This states that the disorder of any closed system will always increase		4
In terms of raw power, *that* would be more than is currently used by the whole of the EU.		8
We need to start doing what we can to avert *that*		10
They are in constant flux		13
That could open the door to enormous efficiency gains		15
These are exactly the kinds of trade-offs non-equilibrium thermodynamics predicts		19

IV Language enhancement

Task 6 Study the words or phrases in the table below and identify them in the text. Try to work out their meanings by using the context in which you find them without using a dictionary. The first one has been done for you.

Word or phrase	Possible meaning	Paragraph
fledgling	immature or underdeveloped	1
hum		2
vie		3
traction		3
sate		3
corral		5
in tandem		6
malfunction		7
balloon		8

(Continued)

Word or phrase	Possible meaning	Paragraph
hard-won		18
hamstring		21

V Reading skills: Identifying the logical order

Task 7 Put the sentences in the table below in a logical order to form a new paragraph. Make use of lexical clues to help you.

Sentence	Number
That is an unavoidable consequence of how they work, and to understand why, we have to think about what computers do.	
Computers do that in the form of bits: fundamental units of digital information that can adopt one of two states, either a 0 or a 1.	
Anyone who has ever sat with a laptop on his knees knows computers give off heat.	
These are represented in computers by tiny electronic switches called transistors that flick on and off when a voltage is applied.	
This process generates electrical resistance in computer chips, which manifests as heat.	
Broadly speaking, they are machines capable of storing and manipulating information.	
Given that modern computer chips feature billions of transistors working together, this can raise the temperature considerably.	

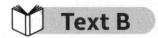

Analogue Comeback

Anna Demming

1 Amid an epic haul of jewels and statues rescued from an ancient Greek shipwreck, it was a lump of corroded wood and bronze that would capture the world's imagination. Pulled from the Mediterranean Sea in 1901, the Antikythera mechanism was an astonishingly sophisticated 2,000-year-old computer. The size of a shoebox, sporting chunky bronze gears rimmed with hundreds of triangular teeth, it was built to chart the paths of celestial bodies and was capable of addition, multiplication, subtraction and division—all by cranking a handle.

2 Nearly half a century would pass before its significance became apparent. By that time, the world had developed a new breed of calculators: the digital computers we still use today. Powered by electricity rather than a hand crank, they were a huge step forward and have proved fast and powerful enough to keep the modern world afloat.

3 But digital computers aren't always the best tool for the job. Much of the mathematics used at the frontiers of modern science, for example, translates awkwardly into digital technology, where certain equations are cumbersome to solve. New approaches are increasingly sought after in the design of artificial intelligence, too, where digital computers struggle to mimic the complex processes of the human brain. As such, the latest hardware is often too expensive and inefficient to use in this area.

4 Mechanical devices are unlikely to be the answer. Even so, to better meet today's challenges, researchers at the cutting edge of computer development are looking to analogue techniques that have more in common with the Antikythera mechanism than today's conventional computers. To save computing's future, we may need a blast from the past.

5 As the name suggests, analogue computers can provide a physical analogue of the system they are describing. In a device like the Antikythera mechanism that is made up of a set of rotating cogs, for example, the positions of certain cogs represent the locations of the sun and moon. You can always tell where those objects are just by looking at the cogs.

6 By contrast, a digital machine has no such exact mappings. Instead, it converts all information to numbers, such as the coordinates of the sun and moon, and performs

calculations on those numbers to chart their change. By operating on the numbers independently of how the physical equipment itself works, digital computing can be hugely versatile. Swapping between different problems just means setting up a different set of mathematical commands, rather than re-engineering cogs or their equivalent for each type of calculation.

A Little Bit Better

7   A key characteristic of digital computers is the use of binary digits—also known as bits—that represent all the processed or stored data as a string of 0s and 1s. In the first digital computers, information was stored and fed in via punch cards with holes representing 0s and solid card representing 1s. For the calculation itself, the computers read the information and translate it onto circuits equipped with transistors capable of switching between two states—that is, routing a current one way or another. Processing the data then involves following a program that flips the right set of switches at each stage of the calculation.

8   One drawback of storing data in the form of binary digits is that the values for variables are no longer continuous. Whereas a pointer on a cog can rotate seamlessly through everything between the numbers 4 and 5, for instance, a basic digital computer might jump from 4.1 to 4.2 without being able to represent the values in between. Adding more bits can make the gaps between numbers ever smaller, but having to make jumps of some size is inevitable.

9   This doesn't necessarily mean a drop in accuracy. Think of a digital stopwatch versus an analogue one: Although a precise measurement of the angle of the second hand could, in theory, allow you to read off infinitely small units of time, in reality the eye won't read a simple dial with the same accuracy that digital figures can drill down to.

10   The first programmable, general-purpose digital computer was the Electronic Numerical Integrator and Computer (ENIAC), introduced in 1946. It was the size of a room and took days to program, but it was significantly more powerful than any computer that had come before. Analogue approaches kept up for a while, but they were little more than a quaint memory by the 1980s.

11   Yet even today the world isn't as digital as it seems. "The physical world is analogue," says Yannis Tsividis at Columbia University in New York. Analogue technology is still all around us. The electromagnetic radio signals that our smartphones use to communicate with each other, for instance, are analogue, requiring analogue-to-digital converters to allow the phone's digital electronics to process them.

12   Analogue isn't just useful for shifting data from one place to another. There are situations where these technologies are proving superior to digital ones for processing data, too. One key area concerns the kinds of equations used for everything from modelling the effects of hormone levels in the body to understanding particle behaviour. These differential and integral equations are mathematical expressions in which quantities are related in terms of their rate of change rather than just their values. The digital approach to tackling them involves calculating and storing the value of each point along a function relating two variables, and then performing calculations on those stored values. An analogue computer, by contrast, would be able to work on the whole function at once.

13   One way of doing this is to harness the mathematics that governs electrical circuits themselves. Quantities like electric current, charge and capacitance are related by rates of change in their values. This means they fit differential equations, allowing electrical circuits to serve as analogues for all other systems governed by such mathematical expressions. That is why Tsividis and his colleagues have used these kinds of circuit elements to develop all-electrical analogue chips.

14   Unlike the analogue computers of the 1940s and 1950s, with their punch cards and primitive wiring, these chips benefit from all the same advances in semiconductor research that have made digital computers smaller and faster. These new analogue chips can connect to each other as well as to conventional digital computers, and—most importantly—can solve certain problems faster and more efficiently than their digital counterparts. For example, multiplying two eight-digit binary values digitally would take about 3,000 transistors, but an analogue computer would need a maximum of eight. "People did not seem to have considered analogue computing in the context of modern technology," says Tsividis. "We did, and things looked very promising."

15   It isn't only electronics that could be useful for analogue computing. Researchers are now turning to beams of light, not least because of the possibility of superfast data transfer. Optical technology offers other benefits as well. When you put objects in the way of light, for example, you get effects that provide a physical analogue for a wide range of phenomena. These range from simple dispersion—which can also be used to describe the behaviour of electrons—to solitons, lone travelling waves that share mathematical descriptions with earthquakes and stock market behaviour.

16   Nader Engheta at the University of Pennsylvania and his colleagues have shown that fast optical analogue computing is possible using interactions between light and matter. They have used a complex structure known as a metamaterial to affect the path of light in such a way that it can solve integral equations. Their prototype, which

looks like a Swiss cheese about half a metre or so across, is designed to work on the long wavelengths of microwave radiation. Future iterations could do so on optical or shorter wavelength radiation, allowing the structure to be a thousand times smaller and faster.

Brain Training

17   One particularly influential backer of analogue computing has been the U.S. Defense Advanced Research Projects Agency (DARPA), which invests in innovative technology. In 2016, DARPA sought designs for analogue or hybrid analogue/digital devices that could provide the capabilities of a supercomputer in a desktop device. Some of the most promising ideas to come out of that scheme revolved around electronic devices called memristors.

18   Any time an electric current flows through a circuit, it encounters resistance. In a memristor, that resistance changes in response to previous use, and the altered resistance state is retained when the circuit is off, meaning it has memory. This is useful for computing as power-free data storage, but also interests scientists working on neuromorphic computing, in which electronic circuits are used to mimic the workings of a brain.

19   The strength of the connections, or synapses, between the brain's neurons grows stronger as more signals pass through them and weakens if signals become rare, giving them learning functions akin to muscle memory. This continuously varying connectivity is awkward to replicate with digital technology, which needs currents to be in one state or another—on or off. Memristors are therefore seen as an attractive basis for neuromorphic computing.

20   Not everyone is convinced. "I see some marginal benefits of analogue circuits for neuromorphic implementations, but these benefits come with very high costs that are generally not worth paying," says Mike Davies, director of Intel's Neuromorphic Computing Lab. "Digital design methods optimise the key figures of merit that matter—accuracy, power, speed and chip cost—in ways that analogue approaches can't match."

21   Few would argue that digital generally wins hands down in terms of precision. What seems to still be open to debate is how much that matters. "These [analogue] devices and systems emulate real neural-processing systems," says Giacomo Indiveri at the Swiss Federal Institute of Technology in Zurich. "As such, they are noisy, imprecise and unreliable." Indiveri is an advocate for combining analogue with digital technologies to get the best from both. His view is that what biological neural-processing systems lack in precision, they make up for with sophisticated feedback mechanisms for adaptation,

learning and plasticity. Designed correctly, neuromorphic devices and algorithms could also benefit from this trade-off.

22 That could have huge implications for the power and speed of computing. The tech giant IBM's Blue Gene was one of the most powerful supercomputers in the world in 2011, yet it still struggled to simulate the billions of neurons and synapses in the brain of a cat, all while guzzling through enough energy to run a thousand domestic homes.

23 Memristor devices could not only be more compact, but stand a chance of matching the brain's energy efficiency, delivering the same results on a thousandth of the power. As ever more objects, from smart fridges to children's toys, become equipped with computational power as part of the much-touted Internet of things, Indiveri sees analogue-embracing hybrid technologies as a way to power these devices more efficiently.

24 He isn't alone. IBM has teams dedicated to analogue innovation for AI. One of the firm's researchers, Hsinyu Tsai, points out that such analogue devices are already finding use in everyday technology, such as the specialized chips that let you rouse your phone with a spoken command. "Analogue approaches fit especially well with today's AI applications, where models consist of a large number of computations, yet require only limited numerical precision," says Tsai.

25 It was two thousand years ago that the Antikythera mechanism sank to the sea floor. After all this time, perhaps we are only just coming to understand the true power of its analogue legacy. (*New Scientists*, July 25, 2020)

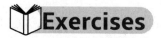

I Fast reading

Task 1 Tick (√) the statement that most closely reflects the writer's point of view.

(   ) A. The Antikythera mechanism was an astonishingly sophisticated 2,000-year-old computer.

(   ) B. Researchers are looking to analogue techniques that have more in common with the Antikythera mechanism to solve some cumbersome equations.

UNIT **4** Computing Science

(　) C. Studies have shown that fast optical analogue computing is possible using interactions between light and matter.

(　) D. Scientists work on neuromorphic computing, in which electronic circuits are used to mimic the workings of a brain.

II Annotating skills

Task 2 Read Paragraphs 1–6, identify which functions the following paragraphs have, complete the table below using the annotations you have made, and find key information in relevant paragraphs as extra comment. The first one has been done for you.

- background information
- general problem
- solution
- exemplification
- cause
- explication
- implication
- evaluation
- viewpoint
- definition
- transition
- summary
- comparison & contrast
- conclusion

Paragraph(s)	Function	Extra comment
1-2	background information	the Antikythera mechanism, the digital computers
3		
4		
5–6		

III Reading for specific information

Task 3 Read Text B carefully, but as fast as you can. Try to answer as many questions as you can without referring to the text.

1. How did the Antikythera mechanism work?

2. Why are researchers looking to analogue techniques that have in common with the Antikythera mechanism?

3. How do computers store and process data by using binary digits?

4. What is the disadvantage of binary digits?

5. Why are researchers turning to optical analogue computing?

6. What did DARPA do with analogue computing?

7. What is a memristor?

8. What does Davies say about the memristor?

9. What does Indiveri advocate and why?

10. What does Tsai think of analogue techniques?

IV Language enhancement

Task 4 Study the words or phrases in the table below and identify them in the text. Try to work out their meanings by using the context in which you find them without using a dictionary. The first one has been done for you.

Word or phrase	Possible meaning	Paragraph
corroded	gradually destroyed by a machine or by rust	1
breed		2
dial		9
function		12
harness		13
charge		13
akin to		19
win hands down		21
guzzling		22

UNIT 4 Computing Science

V Reading skills: Making notes—mind map

Task 5 In Text B, the writer has explained some advantages and disadvantages about the digital technology and the analogue techniques. Check the text to complete the mind map below.

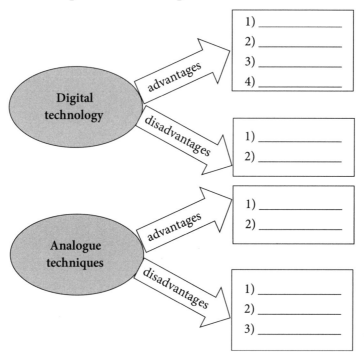

UNIT 5

Food Science

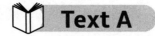

Making Life Look and Taste Better

Ralph Early

Introduction

① Food can be an emotive subject. We live in an age when our modern food marketplace is overwhelmed with products as never before, which can and often does make wise food choices something of a challenge. This can be especially so when the complexity of products transcends consumers' understanding of manufacturing methods and the function of food ingredients and additives. When faced with a knowledge deficit concerning food products, consumers invariably place their trust in those who make and sell foodstuffs to protect their interests, for instance, concerning the assurance of authenticity and food safety. This does not mean, however, that consumers will not express apprehension about the foodstuffs they are offered, or that concerns will not arise from time to time. A clear illustration is seen in the highly impassioned issue of chlorinated chicken, which may be imported into the U.K. from the U.S.A. as part of a Brexit-related trade deal, facilitated by the lowering of U.K. food standards.

② While chlorinated chicken represents a particular and topical point of concern about food, other factors also fuel consumers' anxieties. Of these, one of the most enduring is that of food additives. Indeed, such can be consumers' concerns about these additions to food that the subject has occupied a place at or near the top of consumers' list of uncertainties about food for many decades. So, what exactly are food additives? Are they safe? Who regulates them? What do they do? Why do we use them? This article addresses these questions and provides some insight into the importance of food additives in food science and technology.

1. _____

③ Food additives are substances of natural or synthetic origin which may be added to food for specific technical reasons in order to achieve desired outcomes, e.g. to prevent spoilage and ensure food safety by use of antimicrobial agents or to alter organoleptic properties, such as flavour, colour and mouthfeel with sensory agents. They are typically used in accordance with legal requirements, although the nature of regulation varies from country to country and according to the agreements of trading communities. At a global level, three organizations have been influential in standardising the regulation of food additives: the Joint FAO/WHO Expert Committee on Food Additives (JECFA), the United States Food and Drug Administration (FDA) and the European Food Safety Authority (EFSA).

4 The definition of "food additive" varies among regulatory authorities. For example, in the U.S.A. "indirect food additives", e.g. food contact materials, are included, but "colour additives" are regulated separately. Processing aids are also classed as food additives in the U.S.A., while some other authorities do not consider them so, e.g., the EU. In the U.S.A., a substance intentionally used as a food additive may be classified as "GRAS" (Generally Recognized as Safe) under sections 201(s) and 409 of the Federal Food, Drug, and Cosmetic Act, whereby a substance achieves GRAS status through appropriate scientific procedures, or it was granted such status because it was in use in food before 1958. Within the EU, food additives are governed by Regulation (EC) No 1331/2008 of the European Parliament and of the Council of 16 December 2008.

5 Food additives are classified into six categories (Table 5-1) which define the key functions of the additives allocated to each category and these are further subdivided (Table 5-2), as illustrated by the EU's E number classification system, where the letter "E" prefix for each additive code indicates "Europe". The Codex Alimentarius Commission has established class names and an international numbering system for food additives, based on the EU's code system which allows all food additives, whether approved or not, to be identified by a common means. While the E prefix is used in the EU, it is omitted outside Europe.

Table 5-1 Six Main Categories of Food Additives

Preservatives	Nutritional supplements	Flavouring agents	Colourings	Texturing agents	Miscellaneous
• Antimicrobials • Antibrowning agents • Antioxidants	• Vitamins • Minerals	• Sweeteners • Flavour enhancers • Other flavours	• Carotenoids • Dyes of various colours	• Stablisers • Emulsifiers	• Enzymes • Catalysers • Solvents • Propellants

Table 5-2　Example Ice Cream Ingredients Lists

Dairy ice cream
Cream, skimmed milk, sugar, egg yolk, vanilla.
Soft scoop ice cream (based on U.K. ingredients declarations)
Skimmed milk concentrate, sugar, glucose syrup, coconut oil, whey powder, dextrose, emulsifier (mono- and diglycerides of fatty acids), stabilisers (locust bean gum, guar gum), flavourings, colours (carotenes, beetroot red).
No sugar low-calorie ice cream (based on U.S. ingredients declarations)
Milk, polydextrose, sorbitol, maltodextrin, sucralose, dessert solids (whey solids, non-fat dry milk), edible salts (sodium carbonate, sodium citrate, dipotassium phosphate), stabiliser (microcrystalline cellulose, cellulose gum, mono and diglycerides, polysorbate 80, guar gum, locust bean gum, carrageenan, maltodextrin), artificial flavour.

2. _____

6　Although consumers today may express concerns about the use of additives in food products, they often overlook the fact that some have been in use for thousands of years. Salt is one of the earliest and most prized. Indeed, the concept of food preservation likely began with salt somewhere alongside the wood smoking of meat, fish and cheese. The harvesting of salt dates back around 8,000 years in China and around 4,000 years ago it was used to preserve fish. The use of salt to preserve soy beans undoubtedly led to the development of soy sauce. The Ancient Egyptians and Phoenicians traded in salt and salt preserved foodstuffs, while the Romans sought rock salt deposits in their conquest of European provinces. During the Neolithic period from the 8th to 5th centuries BC, salt was mined in the Austrian settlement of Hallstatt and the wealth of the Austrian principality of Salzburg, as the name suggests, was built upon the mining of salt. Other early applications of food additives include the use of alum (potassium aluminium sulphate) by the Romans to whiten bread and the Egyptian practice of colouring food with saffron. In early Indian and Chinese civilisations, wall saltpetre ($Ca(NO_3)_2$) was used to cure meat and by the European Medieval period, salt combined with saltpetre ($NaNO_3$) was used to redden and cure meat. This happened beneficially to reduce the risk of botulism, although it was not understood at the time that, e.g. sodium nitrate ($NaNO_3$) is reduced to sodium nitrite ($NaNO_2$), which is bacteriostatic against Clostridium botulinum. Other historical methods of food preservation utilising food additives, which also effect advantageous physical and organoleptic changes with materials such as meats, fruits and vegetables, include increasing osmotic pressure with sugar, acidification with acetic acid as vinegar and the use of alcohol.

⑦ While the traditional use of food additives centred mainly on food preservation, developments in industrial chemistry during the last two centuries brought new possibilities to food science and technology. Importantly, as new food additives became available, they transformed the nature, quality and variety of food products available to consumers. Certainly, many food products would not exist today without the use of food additives. These substances make possible many products ranging from confectionery, snack-foods and convenience foods to ready-to-eat and low-calorie products as well as vegetable fat spreads, etc. One of the most significant early uses of modern food additives was in the nutritional fortification of foodstuffs, as during the early part of the 20th century, the nutritional inadequacy of food was becoming well understood. The fortification of salt with iodine to prevent goitre began in the 1920s and in 1941, bread in the U.K. was fortified with calcium to prevent rickets while the fortification of white and brown flour with iron, thiamine and niacin is legally mandated to compensate for losses during milling.

3. _____

⑧ Food additives which serve as processing agents are invaluable to today's food industry. These materials enable the modification and control of food systems. For instance, egg yolk, which contains the natural emulsifier lecithin, has traditionally been used as an emulsifying agent in the manufacture of ice cream and is still used by some manufacturers. However, cost effective alternatives, such as mono- and diglycerides of fatty acids, are now commonly used (Table 5-2) along with the additives, locust bean gum and guar gum, which provide structure, viscosity and resistance to melt. In an age when consumers may be concerned about calorie intake, ice cream-like products can even be made by creative use of additives to permit the exclusion of fat and sugar (Table 5-2). Other food additives invaluable to food processing include starches, used in a wide range of products to modify texture, regulate viscosity, replace fat, etc. and glycerol, a humectant, used to control moisture in confectionery and baked goods.

⑨ Preservatives are a very important class of food additive; they help to maintain food as fit to eat, thereby reducing waste as well as ensuring food safety. Different preservatives have different functions and choice will be determined by factors such as food system type, fat content, water activity and packaging system as well as whether preservation needs to address chemical change and the use of antioxidants, or microbial activity and the use of antimicrobials. Preservatives such as butylated hydroxyanisole (BHA), butylated hydroxytoluene (BHT) and tocopherols act as antioxidants or free radical scavengers to protect against lipid rancidity. As stated above, the antimicrobials, sodium nitrate and sodium nitrite protect against botulism, but if preventing fungal spoilage is important, then organic acids such as benzoic and propionic acids may be used.

10 Food colourings and food flavourings are invaluable food additives. They can be used to enhance or change the features of a product or to rectify changes which occur when, for example, thermal processing used for preservation causes degradation and loss. Visual acceptability is critical to consumers' acceptance of food and the flavour-aroma complex provides an inducement to repeat purchase. Food colourings and food flavourings have, consequently, become pillars of the modern food industry and indispensable to the existence of some food products. Sweetness is, perhaps, inevitably exploited by some food businesses as a means of attracting consumers given the pleasure humans derive from sweet foodstuffs. However, the use of nutritive sweeteners, such as sugar and glucose-fructose syrup, may give rise to health concerns, e. g. obesity and type 2 diabetes, so, in response, some manufacturers utilise synthetic, non-nutritive sweeteners such as cyclamates, aspartame and acesulfame K to produce low-calorie products.

4. _____

11 There can be no doubt that food additives are essential to the work of the food industry as well as being beneficial to consumers, whose food choices would be limited by their absence. Consumer understanding of the role of food additives may at times be distorted by half-truths and myths perpetuated by social media and complicated by distrust in the food industry and regulatory authorities. The term "food additive" itself can be a source of anxiety for consumers because it conveys a sense of something unknowable to all but scientists, and it may then be intensified by seemingly inaccessible code numbers and/or chemical names on product labels. Actors within the food industry also do little to allay consumers' concerns when voicing arrogant rejoinders that all foods are chemicals, so why worry about food additives? When knowledge and trust are problematic, the food industry and government together bear the moral obligation to put consumers at ease. Information should, as a normative moral obligation on the part of the industry and government, always be available to facilitate consumers' informed consent in matters of food choice and, of course, the moral duty

likewise exists to ensure that any additives used are safe to consume. However, this can be an aspect of food technology where science and politics collide.

12   The joint FAO/WHO Expert Committee on Food Additives is the international body responsible for evaluating the safety of food additives. The work of this committee determines the acceptable daily intake (ADI) for food additives as the level that will not cause harm over a lifetime of consumption. The matter of harm can be complicated by some food additives being considered safe in some countries, but not in others. For example, potassium bromate and azodicarbonamide are permitted leavening agents in baked goods in the U.S.A., but are banned as possible carcinogens by the EU. Similarly, some food colourants permitted in the U.S.A. are not allowed in foods in the EU. Indeed, the colours tartrazine (E102) and quinoline yellow (E104) are among six considered by the UK's Food Standards Agency to be linked to hyperactivity in children.

13   The possibility that the U.K. Government may abandon adherence to the EU's food standards in order to strike Brexit-related trade deals with the U.S.A. itself creates a variety of moral predicaments concerning food safety and food additives. The prospect exists that for political expediency, food considered unsuitable or even unfit for consumption by British citizens due to lack of compliance with once respected EU food standards, will be reclassified as suitable for consumption at the stroke of a pen. Clearly, this is philosophically and intellectually incoherent and the absence of independent scientific and moral appraisal as well as, conceivably, the subordination of consumers' interests—particularly their health and well-being—to political objectives raises questions of human rights.

Conclusions

14   The Food Additives and Ingredients Association uses the phrase "Making Life Look and Taste Better", an expression which captures succinctly the purpose of food additives. So many of the food products we enjoy today do indeed look and taste better because of them and we should not overlook the fact that some foodstuffs naturally contain compounds which, when isolated, are also used as food additives. This is not to say that food additives are necessary to every food product and certainly some food businesses have adopted "clean label" strategies to reduce both ingredients and additives to enhance perceptions of wholesomeness. However, the food marketplace would be a very different place without food additives and our food choices would be very much poorer. (*Food Science and Technology*, September 2020)

Exercises

I Fast reading

Task 1 Tick (√) the statement that most closely reflects the writer's point of view.

(   ) A. Food additive regulation varies from country to country.

(   ) B. Consumers are worried about the use of food additives in food products.

(   ) C. Food additives are essential to the work of food industry.

(   ) D. Although consumers misunderstand the role of food additives, they are important in food science and technology.

Task 2 Match the headings with the numbered blanks within the text.

Heading	Number
Consumer-related Perspectives of Food Additives	
Historical Use of Food Additives	
Food Additive Regulation	
Food Additives Today	

II Annotating skills

Task 3 Identify which functions the following paragraphs of the text have, complete the table below using the annotations you have made, and find key information in relevant paragraphs as extra comment. The first one has been done for you.

- ◆ background information
- ◆ general problem
- ◆ solution
- ◆ exemplification
- ◆ cause
- ◆ explication

UNIT **5** Food Science

- implication
- definition
- comparison & contrast
- evaluation
- transition
- conclusion
- viewpoint
- summary

Paragraph(s)	Function	Extra comment
1	background information	consumers' concerns about food authenticity and safety, especially food additives
2		
3		
4–5		
6–10		
11		
12		
13		
14		

III Reading for specific information

Task 4 Read Text A carefully, but as fast as you can. Try to answer as many questions as you can without referring to the text.

1. When making food choices, whom do consumers place their trust in?

2. Why are food additives added to food?

3. Can you name three influential organizations in standardizing the regulation of food additives?

4. What are the six categories of food additives?

5. Can you introduce the history of one of the earliest food additives?

6. What is the main traditional use of food additives?

7. What are the functions of modern food additives?

8. Why are preservatives an essential class of food additives?

9. What are the functions of food colorings and food flavorings?

10. What may happen if food manufacturers use nutritive sweeteners?

11. Why is consumers' understanding of the role of food additives distorted?

12. Who has the moral obligation to help ease consumers' concerns about food additives?

13. How much do you know about the joint FAO/WHO Expert Committee on Food Additives?

14. Why may the U.K. government abandon adherence to the EU's food standards?

15. What would the food marketplace be like if there were no food additives?

Task 5 Read the text and try to find the text-referring words in the table. Note down the idea or word(s) that each one refers to. The first one has been done for you.

Text-referring word(s)	Refers to...	Paragraph
This can be especially so when the complexity of products transcends consumers' understanding of manufacturing methods	It refers to the former sentence: We live in an age when our modern food marketplace is overwhelmed with products as never before, which can and often does make wise food choices something of a challenge.	1
The subject has occupied a place at or near the top of consumers' list of uncertainties about food for many decades		2
They are typically used in accordance with legal requirements		3

(Continued)

Text-referring word(s)	Refers to...	Paragraph
This happened beneficially to reduce the risk of botulism		6
These materials enable the modification and control of food systems		8
They can be used to enhance or change the features of a product or to rectify changes		10
It may then be intensified by seemingly inaccessible code numbers		11

IV Language enhancement

Task 6 Locate the phrases in the text and complete the table below by explaining the meaning of each italicized word in your own words. Pay attention to the writer's choice of the adjective or adverb for emphasis. The first one has been done for you.

Phrase	Meaning	Paragraph
invariably place their trust in	always	1
highly impassioned issue		1
typically used		3
intentionally used		4
significant early uses		7
invaluable food additives		10
inevitably exploited		10
seemingly inaccessible		11
capture *succinctly*		14
naturally contain		14

Task 7 Locate the words or phrases in the text and try to work out their meanings in context. Think about how the writer uses these words and phrases below and the effect the writer's choice of language has on the reader. The first one has been done for you.

Word or phrase	Meaning	Paragraph
knowledge deficit	insufficient or no awareness of necessary information	1
from time to time		1
fuel consumers' anxieties		2
serve as		8
critical to		10
derive from		10
give rise to		10
allay consumers' concerns		11
put consumers at ease		11
at the stroke of a pen		13
overlook the fact		14

V Reading skills: Making notes—mind map

Task 8 Read Paragraph 6 of Text A about the traditional additives and their functions and complete the mind map below.

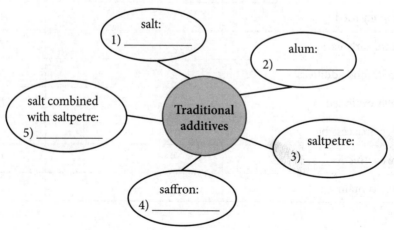

UNIT **5** Food Science

Task 9 Read Paragraphs 7–10 of Text A to identify any further information that could be added to the mind map.

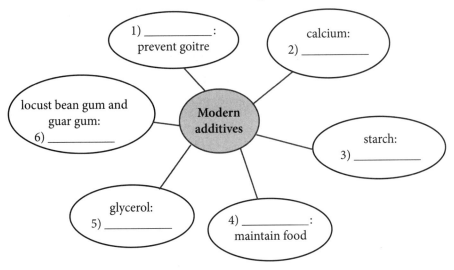

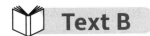

Precision Nutrition

Graham Lawton

❶ For about a decade, geneticist Tim Spector of King's College London ate the same thing every day: a tuna and sweetcorn sandwich on brown bread, followed by a banana. He thought it was a healthy choice, until he turned the microscope on himself and discovered that it was about the worst possible thing he could eat. He was having huge post-lunch surges of sugar and fat in his bloodstream, both of which are known risk factors for diabetes, heart disease and obesity.

❷ But just because tuna sandwiches are bad for Spector doesn't mean they are bad for everyone. Far from it: For some people, they are super healthy. The same is true of almost any food, even things like ice cream and white bread that have long been considered universally bad news.

❸ Recent research by Spector and others has revealed that our response to food is highly individualized and that, consequently, there is no such thing as a healthy diet that works for everybody. In fact, people respond to food in such idiosyncratic ways that everybody needs a personalized nutrition plan. Now he and others, including the U.S. National Institutes of Health, are seeking to deliver such plans in a healthy eating revolution that is being called "precision nutrition". The findings could also explain why decades of one-size-fits-all dietary advice has failed to halt the global epidemic of obesity and diabetes and why nutrition science has consistently failed to produce a straight answer to its most pressing question: What constitutes a healthy diet?

4   The idea of diet as a major determinant of health goes back to at least the ancient world, with Hippocrates' famous (but probably apocryphal) dictum "let food be your medicine". Scientific attempts to define a healthy diet date back to the 1890s, when nutrition pioneer Wilbur Atwater at Wesleyan University in Connecticut published the first ever dietary guidelines. He recommended variety, moderation and the avoidance of too much fat, sugar and starch. That advice has largely stood the test of time, along with its underlying assumption that there is such a thing as a healthy diet. But now, 125 years of nutritional orthodoxy is being chewed up.

5   The first taster of a new paradigm came, as so often happens, from scientists outside the field trying to answer a different question.

6   In 2014, a team at the Weizmann Institute of Science in Israel began probing the effects of artificial sweeteners. Immunologist Eran Elinav and mathematician Eran Segal were specifically interested in whether sweeteners were actually worsening the epidemics of obesity and diabetes that these substances were supposed to be helping to cure. So they and their colleagues fed saccharin to healthy human subjects and watched what happened.

7   One measurement they took was glycaemic response: whether consuming sweeteners caused subjects' blood sugar to rise. This is a normal reaction to eating, but if glucose rises and falls too quickly, or "spikes", it is a marker of poor metabolic health. "People who have regular glucose spikes are more likely to develop diabetes and put on weight than people who don't," says Spector.

Sugar Rush

8   What they saw took them by surprise. In some people, glucose spiked dramatically, some had no spike at all and others were somewhere in the middle. "We saw highly personalised responses," says Elinav. That wasn't supposed to happen for two reasons. First, artificial sweeteners contain no calories so shouldn't cause a spike at all—though why they do is a different story. Second, glycaemic responses aren't supposed to vary much from person to person. There is scope for some individual variation, but people given the same foods are expected to have broadly similar spikes. This is the concept

behind the glycaemic index (GI), a measure of how quickly a given foodstuff is converted into glucose and diffuses into the bloodstream.

9   The unexpected result sent Elinav and Segal back to the original studies on the glycaemic response. "We realised that all of them utilised a very small number of volunteers, maybe 10, who were given identical foods and then had their blood sugar measured," says Elinav. "The average response was turned into the GI for that food. We couldn't find anything on individual responses to foods."

10   So they set out to do that work, and found enormous variation in glycaemic responses to the same foods. In one experiment, they and their colleagues compared industrially produced white bread with artisan wholegrain sour dough, which Elinav describes as "the best bread ever made in Tel Aviv". Based on GI, they expected the white loaf to always generate a bigger glucose spike, but that turned out not to be the case. For some people, mass-produced white bread was healthier than wholegrain sour dough. "We were stunned," says Elinav. "You give people a slice of white bread, some people don't spike at all and others spike to diabetic levels, though on average, they spike to exactly the glycaemic index of white bread. And this is true for almost any food."

11   This was a seminal moment, says Elinav. "It told us something very interesting, but also disturbing: that this paradigm of the one-size-fits-all diet is inherently flawed. If your glycaemic response to a given food is opposite to mine, then the same food cannot be good for both of us. We realized that rather than scoring the foods, maybe we should be scoring the individuals who eat the foods."

12   This finding tallies with that of another study on 800 volunteers led by Elinav and Segal, which is now widely regarded as the foundational paper in precision nutrition. They gathered information on each participant's age, gender, lifestyle and medical history. They measured their body mass index and waist-to-hip ratio and took stool samples to reveal people's microbiomes. Then they monitored the volunteers' blood glucose for a week while getting them to exhaustively log what they ate and when, plus their sleep and activity patterns. In total, the researchers recorded glycaemic responses to more than 52,000 meals. As hinted at by their earlier studies, these were hugely individualized, even after eating identical meals.

13   When they analysed all the data using a machine-learning tool, they found that one of the strongest predictors of an individual's glycaemic response to any given meal was their biometric data, especially microbiome composition. This suggested it should be possible to design a low-GI diet for any individual based on a few measurements.

14   As proof of that pudding, the team then recruited 26 more volunteers, this time

people with prediabetes, ran them through the volley of tests and designed personalized diets. Everyone got a good diet and a bad diet, each of which they ate for a week while being monitored. As hoped, the good diet significantly improved their glucose responses and the bad one made them worse. Yet, unlike the diets that are routinely recommended for people with prediabetes, a number of the good diets contained some pretty unorthodox health foods. "Some people could consume beer or chocolate or ice cream as part of their good diet, but not tomatoes," says Elinav.

15 Since that research, the Weizmann researchers have kept on adding data and have kept on being amazed. "We've now done more than 50,000 individuals and in everyone you encounter surprises," says Elinav. "For some people, some very bad foods are actually very good." Their latest research—as yet unpublished—is the first to look at the long-term effects of a personalised low-GI diet over the course of a year.

16 Other research teams have been doing similar experiments and making similarly surprising discoveries. Spector's group recently published the results of what he says is "the most intensive nutrition intervention study that's been done". PREDICT-1—the Personalized Responses to Dietary Composition Trial—recruited 1,002 healthy people and fed them identical meals for two weeks while keeping track of their lifestyles and measuring their metabolic responses.

Intensive Intervention

17 As well as the glycaemic response, it measured a class of fat called triglycerides, which can also spike in the blood stream after eating. Again, the study found highly individual responses to identical meals. "Some people had hardly any rise, in others it dropped back fast, in others it was going up and up for hours," says Spector. But triglyceride spikes weren't correlated with glucose spikes. "Everyone reacts differently to identical foods," says Spector.

18 Triglycerides are a risk factor for chronic diseases, too. "If you've got all these fats circulating in your blood for long periods of time, it increases inflammation and you get metabolic problems, diabetes, heart disease and obesity."

19 Spector and his team also measured hundreds of baseline variables in the volunteers, including their age, sex, height, weight, body composition, blood pressure, fasting metabolite levels, circadian rhythms, genome sequence, microbiome and normal diet. During the study, the researchers recorded when the participants ate, slept and exercised, and what they ate on top of the standardised meals.

20 After crunching the data with their own machine-learning tool, they found that an aggregate of those measurements could quite accurately predict an individual's

metabolic responses to any given meal. For glycaemic responses, it was 77 percent accurate, and for triglycerides 47 percent. That is far from perfect, but is still progress from merely recommending a universal healthy diet. "We've already moved away from this idea that there's one standard good diet for everybody," says Spector.

21   Separate research led by scientists at Imperial College London arrived at a similar conclusion via another route. They fed people identical diets and analysed thousands of metabolites in their urine. "We find that people respond differently to diet, but we demonstrated it a different way, looking at the metabolic response," says Isabel Garcia-Perez. She and her colleagues are developing a urine test for different "metabotypes" that could be used to personalise people's diets.

22   One big surprise, says Spector, is how little genetics influences responses to food. Among his 1,002 subjects were 86 pairs of identical twins and even they showed widely different responses to the same meal. "That told us straight away that genes don't play a major part," he says. How we respond to a fatty meal has virtually no genetic component and only about 30 percent of our glucose response relates to our genes. Other factors such as gut microbes and circadian rhythms are more important, says Spector.

23   This all holds out the prospect of being able to design personalised diets based on a few simple tests. In the future, maybe you could visit your doctor, donate some blood, stool or urine, take a few tests and go home with a precision diet plan tailored to your individual needs.

24   "We can already do that to some extent," says Spector. "Initially, they're going to be slightly simplistic. But we can already know whether you are someone who should be having more good fats in your diet, whether it's safe to have carbs." His group and the Israeli one are rolling out commercial products that promise to deliver personalized nutrition advice via smartphone apps under the brand names Zoe and The Personalized Nutrition Project. You could also try your own approach.

25   "How effective the apps will be is still up in the air," says Bernadette Moore at the University of Leeds, U.K. Sleep, exercise and the timing of meals also matter, which makes the designing of personalized nutrition plans a complex challenge. The apps will come across the same problems as traditional dietary advice too—people often fail to follow it. But the research holds great promise, she says. The 2015 Israeli study was groundbreaking and had huge implications. "It's a really exciting study and a really exciting space," she says.

26   Yiannis Mavrommatis, who heads the Nutrition and Genetics Research group at St. Mary's University in London, agrees. "The project is a milestone in nutrition science,"

he says. "One of the most impactful findings is confirmation that one-size-fits-all diets will not work for everyone. Personalised nutrition is the natural outcome."

27 Big funders are also getting behind this new field. In May, the U.S. National Institutes of Health announced that precision nutrition would be a research priority over the next 10 years, with a goal to "fundamentally transform nutrition science".

28 One transformation it may deliver is rehabilitation of the flagging reputation of this science. The highly individualized response to foods may be why it so often fails to get its story straight, says Sarah Berry at King's college London. "A lot of people criticise nutritional science. They say we don't know what we're talking about because recommendations are always changing. Actually, that's because food is so complicated and individuals are as complicated."

29 But she warns about taking the new knowledge to extremes. Even though we are moving away from recommending a generic diet, that isn't a licence to disregard all the old advice. "We're not going against the broad-accepted healthy eating guidelines," she says. "We should still all be eating a diverse diet with fibre-rich foods, fruit, veg, nuts and pulses, an appropriate amount of fat and limited processed food. But within this broad spectrum, there is huge potential to personalise to make it even more healthy. It concerns me that some people might say, 'Oh, maybe that means I can eat chocolate all day and I don't need to eat fruit.'"

30 "There are still some high-level paradigms that hold," agrees Elinav. "Calories still matter. Even if ice cream is one of your better foods, if you eat 10 kilos a day, you would still get fat." (*New Scientist*, September 12, 2020)

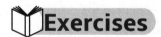

Exercises

I Fast reading

Task 1 Tick (√) the statement that most closely reflects the writer's point of view.

(   ) A. There is huge variation in glycaemic responses to the same foods.

(   ) B. The idea of one standard good diet for everybody is definitely unreasonable, so we should disregard the old food paradigm.

(　　) C. People all respond to the same food in very different ways, so there's no such thing as a healthy diet that works for everyone.

(　　) D. The designing of personalized nutrition plans can be easily worked out.

II Annotating skills

Task 2 Find texts that describe experiments and analyze them in detail. An example has been given for you. Find two more experiments from Text B.

Example:

Immunologist Eran Elinav and mathematician Eran Segal were specifically interested in whether sweeteners were actually worsening the epidemics of obesity and diabetes that these substances were supposed to be helping to cure. So they and their colleagues fed saccharin to healthy human subjects and watched what happened.

One measurement they took was glycaemic response: whether consuming sweeteners caused subjects' blood sugar to rise.

What they saw took them by surprise. In some people, glucose spiked dramatically, some had no spike at all and others were somewhere in the middle. "We saw highly personalised responses," says Elinav. That wasn't supposed to happen for two reasons. First, artificial sweeteners contain no calories so shouldn't cause a spike at all—though why they do is a different story. Second, glycaemic responses aren't supposed to vary much from person to person. There is scope for some individual variation, but people given the same foods are expected to have broadly similar spikes.

This was a seminal moment, says Elinav. "It told us something very interesting, but also disturbing: that this paradigm of the one-size-fits-all diet is inherently flawed. If your glycaemic response to a given food is opposite to mine, then the same food cannot be good for both of us. We realized that rather than scoring the foods, maybe we should be scoring the individuals who eat the foods."

Process of the experiment: Immunologist Eran Elinav, mathematician Eran Segal and their colleagues fed saccharin to healthy human subjects and watched what happened. One measurement they took was glycaemic response: whether consuming sweeteners caused subjects' blood sugar to rise.

Result: In some people, glucose spiked dramatically, some had no spike at all and others were somewhere in the middle.

Evaluation: It told us something very interesting, but also disturbing: that this paradigm of the one-size-fits-all diet is <u>inherently flawed</u>.

1. _____
   _____
   _____
   _____
   _____.

   Process of the experiment: _____
   _____.

   Result: _____
   _____.

   Evaluation: _____
   _____.

2. _____
   _____
   _____
   _____
   _____.

   Process of the experiment: _____
   _____.

   Result: _____
   _____.

   Evaluation: _____
   _____.

III Reading for specific information

Task 3 Read Text B carefully, but as fast as you can. Try to answer as many questions as you can without referring to the text.

1. How did Spector respond to the same food every day?

2. Who was the nutrition pioneer?

UNIT **5** Food Science

3. What did Atwater recommend for diet?

4. What research did the team at the Weizmann Institute of Science in Israel do?

5. What results did the team at the Weizmann Institute of Science in Israel obtain?

6. What did Elinav and Segal's experiment results imply?

7. What was the strongest predictor of an individual's glycaemic response to any given meal according to Elinav and Segal?

8. What is triglyceride?

9. What were the results of research led by scientists at Imperial College London?

10. How does genetics influence people's responses to food?

11. What should people do in the future if they plan to design personalized diets?

12. What could individuals do with smartphone apps under the brand names Zoe and The Personalized Nutrition Project?

13. Why is the designing of personalized nutrition plans a complex challenge?

14. What problems will the apps come across?

15. What is the goal of precision nutrition announced by the U.S. National Institutes of Health?

Task 4 Academic texts often contain quotes from experts within the relevant field. In Text B, the opinions of a number of experts are mentioned. Read the opinions below. Then scan the text for information, matching each opinion to the relevant expert. The first one has been done for you.

Tim Spector   Eran Elinav   Yiannis Mavrommatis   Sarah Berry   Isabel Garcia-Perez

1. People who have regular glucose spikes are more likely to develop diabetes and put on weight than people who don't.   Tim Spector

2. It told us something very interesting, but also disturbing: that this paradigm of the one-size-fits-all diet is inherently flawed. _____

3. We find that people respond differently to diet, but we demonstrated it a different way, looking at the metabolic response. _____

4. That told us straight away that genes don't play a major part. Other factors such as gut microbes and circadian rhythms are more important. _____

5. Initially, they're going to be slightly simplistic. But we can already know whether you are someone who should be having more good fats in your diet, whether it's safe to have carbs. _____

6. One of the most impactful findings is confirmation that one-size-fits-all diets will not work for everyone. Personalized nutrition is the natural outcome. _____

7. A lot of people criticize nutritional science. They say we don't know what we're talking about because recommendations are always changing. Actually, that's because food is so complicated and individuals are as complicated. _____

8. We should still all be eating a diverse diet with fibre-rich foods, fruit, veg, nuts and pulses, an appropriate amount of fat and limited processed food. But within this broad spectrum, there is huge potential to personalize to make it even more healthy. _____

IV Language enhancement

Task 5 Locate the phrases in the text and complete the table below by explaining the meaning of each italicized word in your own words. Pay attention to the writer's choice of the adjective or adverb for emphasis. The first one has been done for you.

Phrase	Meaning	Paragraph
highly individualized	extremely	3
straight answer		3
underlying assumption		4
spike *dramatically*		8
enormous variation		10

UNIT **5** Food Science

(Continued)

Phrase	Meaning	Paragraph
seminal moment		11
foundational paper		12
exhaustively log		12
significantly improved		14
intensive intervention		17
accurately predict		20
widely different		22
flagging reputation		28
huge potential		29

Task 6 Locate the words or phrases in the text and try to work out their meanings in context. Think about how the writer uses these words and phrases below and the effect the writer's choice of language has on the reader. The first one has been done for you.

Word or phrase	Meaning	Paragraph
stand the test of time	be considered valuable by people for many years	4
proof of that pudding		14
the volley of tests		14
keep track of		16
correlate with		17
baseline variable		19
an aggregate of		20
straight away		22
roll out		24
up in the air		25

117

(Continued)

Word or phrase	Meaning	Paragraph
come across		25
hold great promise		25
get its story straight		28

V Reading skills: Inferring meaning

Task 7 Study the words in the table below and identify them in the text. Try to work out their meanings by using the context in which you find them without using a dictionary. The first one has been done for you.

Word	Possible meaning	Paragraph
surge	a sudden onrush or increase	1
idiosyncratic		3
halt		3
orthodoxy		4
probe		6
diffuse		8
tally		12
identical		16
crunch		20
tailor		23
milestone		26
spectrum		29

118

UNIT 6

Archeology

Text A

The Civilization That Time Forgot

David Robson

1　Nearly five and a half millennia ago, a bustling metropolis lay in the delta of the lower Yangtze, in what is now China. You could enter on foot—there was a single road through the towering city walls—but most people travelled by boat via an intricate network of canals. At its heart was a massive palatial complex built on a platform of earth. There were huge granaries and cemeteries filled with elaborately decorated tombs, while the water system was controlled by an impressive series of dams and reservoirs.

2　The inhabitants of this city, known today as Liangzhu, ruled the surrounding flood plains for nearly 1,000 years, their culture extending into the countryside for hundreds of kilometres. Then, around 4,300 years ago, the society quickly declined, and its achievements were largely forgotten. It is only within the past decade that archaeologists have begun to reveal its true importance in world history.

3　Their startling discoveries suggest that Liangzhu was eastern Asia's oldest state-based society, and its infrastructure may even have surpassed the achievements of Egypt and Mesopotamia, thousands of miles to the west. "There's nothing in the world, from my vantage point, that is as monumental in terms of water management—or for that matter, any kind of management—that occurs so early in history," says Vernon Scarborough at the University of Cincinnati in Ohio. One of the biggest chapters in humanity's story, the birth of civilisation, may need to be rewritten.

4　The first evidence of a lost ancient culture in the Yangtze delta was uncovered in 1936, by Shi Xingeng, who worked at the nearby West Lake Museum in Hangzhou. He named the site Liangzhu, after a nearby town. However, the black pottery artefacts he found didn't initially seem remarkable. It was only in the 1970s and 1980s that Liangzhu began to generate much greater excitement, beginning with the excavation of some cemeteries in and around the ancient city.

5　While many of the tombs were rather spartan, with few burial goods, some contained hundreds of beautiful jade objects, including the earliest examples of China's iconic *cong* vessels and delicate *bi* discs. Many of these artefacts were engraved with the image of a man wearing an enormous, plumed headdress, who appears to be riding a large, fanged monster—a motif that could represent a mythical or religious story. The graves also held ceremonial axes, pendants, and plaques depicting the same mythical figures, which seem to have been attached to headgear. These kinds of objects had previously been assigned to much later periods, starting with the Zhou Dynasty in 1046 BC, but here they were, in a 5,000-year-old, Neolithic burial place. It was the first sign that Liangzhu may have been a complex society, with workers producing costly and time-consuming artwork and a social elite rich enough to pay for it.

6   Later digs, inspired by these discoveries, revealed a huge earthen platform at the heart of the city. It is more than 9 metres high and covers 300,000 square metres, and appears to have supported a large palatial complex with buildings made of wood and bamboo, which the researchers named Mojiaoshan. Then came signs of city walls, more than 20 metres wide and often accompanied by internal and external moats. There was obviously an abundance of food too: One pit in the city contains more than 10,000 kilograms of burnt rice from a local granary.

7   Then, in December 2017, a bombshell paper revealed the full extent of the society's hydraulic engineering. Using a combination of satellite photography, coring and excavations, the team led by researchers at the Zhejiang Provincial Institute of Cultural Relics and Archaeology uncovered a series of low-lying levees, built on swampy ground to control the flooding of the alluvial plain, and six "high dams" further upstream, creating reservoirs at the feet of the surrounding mountains.

City of Canals

8   Together, the dams controlled the water flow in more than 10,000 hectares of land and were capable of holding back nearly 6.5 billion cubic metres of water. Carbon dating, plus an analysis of jade artefacts found near the levees, suggests that some of these dams were in operation 5,200 years ago, near the beginning of Liangzhu's existence. And they were built to last: The Qiuwu high dam is still in use today.

9   Besides allowing Liangzhu's citizens to irrigate their paddy fields and control flooding after storm surges, the reservoirs fed 51 waterways. Made from natural river courses and artificial ditches, these canals were about 30 kilometres long in total. "Internal communication within the town must have been largely by boat; this was a town of canals as much as of roads," noted Colin Renfrew at the University of Cambridge and Bin Liu at Zhejiang Provincial Institute of Cultural Relics and Archaeology in a 2018 paper. Perhaps the closest comparison is medieval Venice or one of the "water towns" around Shanghai that emerged thousands of years after Liangzhu and that attract tourists to this day.

10   The canal system was also used to transport building materials, including timber

and rocks, down from the nearby mountains and into the city through its eight water gates. Foundations for the city walls, for instance, appear to come from mountains to the north. "These stones were not quarried per se using tools to cause physical breakage, but collected from the surface," says Yijie Zhuang at University College London, a co-author on the 2017 paper.

11 While research in Liangzhu continues apace, discoveries elsewhere in China indicate that the civilisation's rise was part of a broader social and cultural revolution. Recent archaeological studies show that, starting more than 5,000 years ago, many settlements were emerging in the lower and middle Yangtze regions, in what is now Sichuan Province and along the lower Yellow River. Some, including Shijiahe in the middle Yangtze, are large enough to have required organised labour to build their moats and walls. "Liangzhu is by far the biggest, but you find other walled urban centres," says Jessica Rawson at the University of Oxford. "And you get high levels of craftsmanship, not just in jade, but in several types of ceramics, in several parts of China." There will have been communication between some of these sites, with the larger settlements acting as local power hubs. Liangzhu's cultural influence, for instance, can be found in rural sites more than 100 kilometres away.

12 This paints a very different picture from the traditional view of Chinese history. Small rice-farming communities began to appear around 10,000 years ago. Until recently, however, it was thought that the first Chinese state society—one with a formal political system and complex social organisation—emerged just 3,600 years ago, with the rise of the Shang Dynasty in the Central Plains. But Liangzhu, far to the southeast, has many of the features of a state society around 1,700 years earlier, argue Renfrew and Liu, who has conducted much of the archaeological research at the site.

Hallmarks of State

13 First, there is the size of the population. Liu's team estimates that this peaked at between 22,900 and 34,500, which is many times larger than any earlier Chinese community. Then there is clear evidence of a strict social hierarchy, such as the vast differences between the tombs of the rich and the poor. Finally, there is the ambition of the communal works, including the building of the city walls, the Mojiaoshan platform and palatial complex, and the sophisticated hydraulic engineering.

14 The construction work is particularly impressive when you consider that the city's inhabitants had no pack animals, such as horses or donkeys, or oxen to pull a plough, says Rawson. Nevertheless, they were able to relieve enough people from their agricultural duties to build these monumental structures. "Everything is dependent

on human labour," says Rawson. "And the key thing then is to organise that labour." Liu's team has estimated that constructing the dams alone would have required the movement of around 2.9 million cubic metres of earth, which would have taken 3,000 workers eight years to complete. This was a huge undertaking of the kind that can only come from a sophisticated society with central organisation and planning. "You can't think of this hydraulic project without planning," says Rawson. "This is not a small group of people—this is large-scale management."

15 Even on a global scale, Liangzhu's waterworks were truly groundbreaking. The Middle East is often considered the cradle of civilisation, with a handful of urban societies, such as Tell Brak and Uruk in Mesopotamia, emerging in the fourth millennium BC. These cities had developed water management technology, but their engineering didn't match that of Liangzhu in size or complexity. As Liu and Renfrew put it: "[Liangzhu's dams] maybe the earliest communal works achieved anywhere in the world on such a scale." Scarborough agrees. He visited the site in 2017 and was awestruck by how the citizens of Liangzhu had completely reshaped their environment. "It's an engineered landscape that is second to none, given its antiquity."

16 There is just one surprising absence at Liangzhu. So far, archaeologists have failed to find clear evidence of writing, which is sometimes considered a prerequisite of a fully formed state society. However, it is possible that some symbols found on the pottery and jade aren't simply decorative. Chunfeng Zhang at the East China Normal University in Shanghai says they have some linguistic features. Some of the 656 symbols documented so far are highly standardised in form, and many regularly appear across different sites at the same points on certain artefacts, such as the leg or mouth of a vessel. This suggests they may have a consistent meaning, like a label. Zhang also points to apparent rules in how certain symbols are constructed, which may have changed their meaning. These include the addition of new strokes and the systematic combination of different motifs, which again hints at a nascent writing system. "Some symbols have only decorative functions, some of them represent meaning and for some of them it is difficult to determine the function," she says.

17 Zhang hopes we may one day find the equivalent of a Rosetta Stone to decipher the symbols at Liangzhu. Even without one, the culture rivals other very early societies. With further research, Liangzhu might even shed light on the processes that led humanity to develop complex urban societies. The move from a hunter-gatherer to a farming lifestyle is one known force for the establishment of early settlements, as groups began to congregate around fields. Eventually, farmers pooled resources, collaboration and cooperation increased, and communities grew. But what pushes a society to make the final

leap to a large urban centre with more advanced technology, architecture and politics?

18   Scarborough argues that environmental uncertainty played a central role in Liangzhu. This included the risk of flooding in the wet season, and drier periods that would have destroyed the paddy fields. This uncertainty might first have encouraged the establishment of more regular religious practices that brought dispersed groups together for ceremonies. The depictions of a fearsome monster on artefacts across the region suggest the existence of some kind of shared mythology. Organised religious practices may, in turn, have encouraged the establishment of stricter social norms and even leadership roles for people who seemed able to predict or control the weather, for instance.

19   The formation of a social hierarchy could then have helped to mobilise a large workforce for more practical communal projects such as dam building. While this would have brought greater cohesion and prosperity for the whole community, it would also have helped to cement the elite's power by allowing them to control who had access to the technology and who could enter or leave the city by its canals. The result was a society with a formal government, and with sufficient wealth to create elaborate artwork and architecture.

20   Scarborough believes environmental uncertainty played a key role in the formation of civilisations in the Middle East too—although the main threat there was drought. "It was more the rerouting of a limited amount of water off the Tigris or Euphrates to accommodate the sizeable cities that were beginning to spring up," he says. In each case, the need to control the environment prompted greater cooperation and also gave power to an elite, promoting a new kind of social organisation. "Water [management] is not the only trigger for social complexity, but it's certainly a primary one," he says.

21   If flooding was a trigger that set Liangzhu's development in motion, it may also have been its downfall. Analysing layers of sediment in the region, Zhanghua Wang at the East China Normal University and her colleagues found evidence of repeated marine flooding beginning around 4,500 years ago, with deposits of algae and small marine fossils directly on top of the layers associated with the Liangzhu culture. The damage caused by the flooding, and the increased salinity would have made rice cultivation more and more difficult throughout the region, she says, undermining "the most important economic and social foundation of the Liangzhu society".

22   While the society itself collapsed, its influence appears to have lingered as the inhabitants moved to other parts of what is now China. Liu and others believe that elements of Liangzhu's culture, such as the design of its jade congs, were borrowed and adopted by later societies. And the local landscape has forever been changed by the impressive hydraulic engineering. Flooding might have spelled the end of life in the city

but its citizens left an indelible mark. And, with the ongoing archaeological excavations, this amazing culture is changing our ideas about the dawn of civilisation. (*New Scientist*, March 21, 2020)

I Fast reading

Task 1 Tick (√) the statement that most closely reflects the writer's point of view.

(   ) A. The infrastructure in Liangzhu surpasses the achievements of Egypt and Mesopotamia.

(   ) B. Archaeological research in Liangzhu uncovered many impressive discoveries.

(   ) C. The discovery of a stunning culture in Liangzhu that rivals ancient Egypt and Mesopotamia is rewriting human history.

(   ) D. The environmental uncertainty played a central role in Liangzhu's rise and fall.

II Annotating skills

Task 2 Read text A and complete the following table of text organization.

Part	Paragraph(s)	Main idea
1	Para(s). _____	1) _____ _____.
2	Para(s). _____	Liangzhu was a city of 2) _____. The sophisticated 3) _____ here was impressive and used in many ways. The archaeological research at Liangzhu and other sites showed a different picture of 4) _____, which tells that 5) _____ began to appear 6) _____,

125

(Continued)

Part	Paragraph(s)	Main idea
		and with the features of 7) _____, Liangzhu may be the 8) _____ Chinese state society instead of 9) _____ Dynasty.
3	Para(s). ____	A state society has 10) _____. Liangzhu, as one, had some of the features. In its development and downfall, 11) _____ played a key role.
4	Para(s). ____	In sum, archaeological discoveries in Liangzhu point to a previously unknown civilization and 12) _____.

Task 3 Identify which functions the following parts of the text have, complete the table below using the annotations you have made, and find key information in relevant paragraphs as extra comment. The first one has been done for you.

- background information
- general problem
- solution
- exemplification
- cause
- explication
- implication
- evaluation
- viewpoint
- definition
- transition
- summary
- comparison & contrast
- conclusion

Part	Function	Extra comment
1	background information + viewpoint	general information of archaeological discoveries and history, scholar and author's opinion of the discoveries
2		
3		

UNIT **6** Archeology

(Continued)

Part	Function	Extra comment
4		

III Reading for specific information

Task 4 Read Text A carefully, but as fast as you can, and then try to complete the diagram of the brief archaeological history of Liangzhu.

In 1) _____   2) _____ of Liangzhu culture was uncovered by 3) _____.

In 4) _____ and 5) _____   Some 6) _____ were excavated.

In later digs   At the heart of the city, a huge 7) _____ was revealed, which supported a large 8) _____ named 9) _____ by researchers. Then, came signs of 10) _____.

In 2017   The full extent of the society's 11) _____ was revealed, which consisted of a series of 12) _____ and six 13) "_____".

Task 5 Read text A carefully, but as fast as you can. Try to answer as many questions as you can without referring to the text.

1. How long ago did the Liangzhu culture appear? And when did Liangzhu society quickly decline?

2. In terms of achievements in infrastructure, which country and area may Liangzhu have surpassed?

3. What was the first sign that Liangzhu may have been a complex society?

4. What's the huge earthen platform at the heart of the city like?

5. How long ago were some of the dams already in operation? Which one of them is still in use today?

6. What was the hydraulic engineering used for?

7. How do scholars Colin Renfrew and Bin Liu think of Liangzhu?

8. The writer analyzes Liangzhu as a state society based on a general theory. What are the core elements of the theory?

9. How do Colin Renfrew and Bin Liu comment on Liangzhu's dams?

10. What is considered as a prerequisite of a fully formed state society? According to Chunfeng Zhang, what has linguistic features in Liangzhu's culture?

11. What role did environmental uncertainty play in Liangzhu? What was the element that triggered Liangzhu's rise and fall?

Task 6 Read the text and try to find the text-referring words in the table. Note down the idea or word(s) that each one refers to. The first one has been done for you.

Text-referring word(s)	Refers to...	Paragraph
Their startling discoveries suggest that Liangzhu was eastern Asia's oldest state-based society	archaeologists'	3
The graves also held ceremonial axes, pendants, and plaques depicting *the same mythical figures*		5
These kinds of objects had previously been assigned to much later periods		5
Later digs, inspired by *these discoveries*, revealed a huge earthen platform at the heart of the city		6
the civilisation's rise was part of a broader social and cultural revolution		11

UNIT 6 Archeology

(Continued)

Text-referring word(s)	Refers to...	Paragraph
This paints a very different picture from the traditional view of Chinese history		12
The construction work is particularly impressive		14
This was a huge undertaking		14
but *their engineering* didn't match that of Liangzhu in size or complexity		15
This suggests they may have a consistent meaning		16
This uncertainty might first have encouraged the establishment of more regular religious practices		18
While *the society* itself collapsed		22

IV Language enhancement

Task 7 Find the word(s) in the text with the same or similar meaning(s) to each of the expressions in the left column of the table below. The first one has been done for you.

Expression	Synonym(s) in text	Paragraph(s)
a whole structure (as a building) made up of related structures	complex	1
to make visible		2, 7
a state of human society that is very developed and organized		3
a place for the burial of a dead body		4, 5
proof/confirmation		4
the act of digging		7
to show that something is true or exists		11
a place that is used for something		11

(Continued)

Expression	Synonym(s) in text	Paragraph(s)
related to the study of cultures of the past, and of periods of history by examining the remains of buildings and objects found in the ground		12
moved or operated or effected by liquid (water or oil)		13
the activity of applying scientific knowledge to the design, building and control of machines, roads, bridges, electrical equipment, etc.		13
a task or project, especially one that is important and/or difficult		14
hydraulic engineering		15
a system, especially in a society or an organization, in which people are organized into different levels of importance from the highest to the lowest		19
matter that has been deposited by some natural process		21

Task 8 Locate the words or phrases in the text and try to work out their meanings in context. Think about how the writer uses these words and phrases below and the effect the writer's choice of language has on the reader. The first one has been done for you.

Word or phrase	Possible meaning	Paragraph
via	by means of	1
impressive		1
surpass		3
from my vantage point		3
pottery		4
time-consuming		5
levee		7

(Continued)

Word or phrase	Possible meaning	Paragraph
dam		7
groundbreaking		15
prerequisite		16
shed light on		17
cement		19
spring up		20
indelible		22

V Reading skills: Making notes—mind map

Task 9 Read Text A and complete the mind map below.

Intend to argue
Liangzhu culture is 1) _____ human history
Need to explain

Why   Why

In China:
- Liangzhu is 2) _____ years earilier than the Shang Dynasty, which is traditionally viewed as the first state society.
- Beautiful jade objects, including China's iconic 3) _____ vessels and 4) _____ discs, which had previously been assigned to as early as the 5) _____ Dynasty.

Across the world:
Liangzhu's infrastructure may have 6) _____ the achievements of 7) _____ and 8) _____.
Liangzhu was a city of canals, whose 9) _____ were truly groundbreaking.

Conceive the 10) _____ of the article

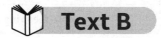

Text B

The First Urbanites

Laura Spinney

1. Around 6,200 years ago, farmers living on the eastern fringes of Europe, in what is now Ukraine, did something inexplicable. They left their neolithic villages and moved into a sparsely inhabited area of forest and steppe. There, in an area roughly the size of Belgium between the modern cities of Kiev and Odessa, they congregated at new settlements up to 20 times the size of their old ones.

2. This enigmatic culture, known as the Cucuteni-Trypillia, predates the earliest known cities in Mesopotamia, a civilisation that spanned part of the Middle East. It persisted for 800 years, but then, as mysteriously as it had begun, this experiment in civilisation failed. The inhabitants left the lightest of footprints in the landscape, and no human remains have been found. "Not a pinkie, not a tooth," says palaeogeneticist Alexey Nikitin at Grand Valley State University in Michigan.

3. This puzzling lack of evidence has fuelled a lively debate about what Nikitin calls the "Dark Ages" of European prehistory. "You talk to five Trypillian archaeologists, you get five different opinions," he says.

4. But the data gap has not stifled interest—quite the opposite. Several projects in recent years have tried to make sense of the Trypillian proto-cities. Despite big disagreements, what is emerging is a picture of an early and unique attempt at urbanisation. It may be the key to understanding how modern Europe emerged from the Stone Age—and even throw new light on the emergence of human civilisation in general.

5. Uruk and Tell Brak, which arose in Mesopotamia early in the 4th millennium BC, are usually considered the world's first cities. Their excavated remains point to an increased density of habitation and a novel, hierarchical social structure—two features that are considered integral to the definition of a city. The idea is that as human populations grew, strangers had to come together in a shared space and get along. "I think that was the real psychological threshold of urbanism," says Monica Smith at the University of California, Los Angeles, an anthropologist and author of *Cities: The First 6,000 Years*. But the Trypillian megasites do not meet either of those criteria, so how should we make sense of them?

6   Ukrainian archaeologists have known about the megasites for more than a century, but systematic excavations did not get under way until after the Second World War, and the sites only came to international attention a decade ago. Today, of the several thousand known Trypillian settlements, around 15 count as "mega" because they cover more than 1 square kilometre. The biggest, Taljanki, is over three times that size, making it slightly larger than London's financial heart, and bigger than Uruk throughout most of the 4th millennium BC.

7   Although sizable, the megasites were not densely populated. They were laid out concentrically, with houses made of wattle and daub lining ring roads circling a large central space. The biggest sites had several thousand houses and as many as 15,000 inhabitants—compared with no more than a few hundred people in a typical neolithic village. There is a heated debate over numbers, though that, in part, is because it is not clear whether the sites were fully inhabited year round. This raises another question: What were these places for?

8   Some take a traditional view. Archaeologist Mykhailo Videiko at Borys Grinchenko Kyiv University, Ukraine, thinks the megasites were simply a response to growing population pressure. The Trypillians' move may have been facilitated by developments in technology, he says, notably the advent of sledges drawn by bulls or other animals. These made it possible to transport food and other resources over a dozen or more kilometres, from existing villages or outlying fields to the new sites. "There were no roads," he says. "This was a landscape of forests and river valleys."

9   Johannes Müller at Kiel University, Germany, views the megasites as essentially overgrown villages—an experiment, yes, but only in scale. The concentric design was not new, he points out: "You see it from around 4800 BC, in older settlements with no more than 50 houses." But John Chapman and Bisserka Gaydarska at Durham University, U.K., could not disagree more. "It's like saying that an aircraft carrier is a very large yacht," says Chapman.

10   For Chapman and Gaydarska, it really was an experiment in social organisation—and the appearance of the megasites reflects this ideological shift. Each was laid out in quarters that radiated from the centre roughly in the shape of pie slices, and further subdivided into neighbourhoods comprising a handful of houses. The overall layout seems to have been imposed from the start, though the quarters took on internal structure gradually, as people moved in. Often, neighbourhoods had their own assembly house, strategically placed on a ring road. A bigger one served each quarter, and there was one, very large meeting house for the site as a whole, near the centre and facing east. These structural subdivisions might have helped contain disputes, says Gaydarska, and

the assembly houses could have been where decisions were made and communicated, at a time before writing was invented. "Trypillian sites were basically egalitarian," says Chapman. "There's very little evidence of prestige goods or elites."

Why Congregate?

11 These were cities, in other words, but of a very different kind from those conceived by the hierarchical, slave-owning societies of Mesopotamia a few centuries later. And that being the case, argue Gaydarska and Chapman, our definition of a city needs expanding.

12 Others don't go quite as far. Smith calls the megasites "collective settlements", and suggests we might think of them as immediate precursors of cities, where people who only knew the small-scale, egalitarian village life had their first taste of something bigger and more heterogeneous. "They could be capturing something of that transition," she says. In fact, she thinks the megasites may have had something in common with Göbekli Tepe in modern Turkey, a building complex which is at least 10,000 years old and seems to have been a place where people congregated periodically to observe rituals. It might have been at such pilgrimage centres that the idea of unfamiliarity—of the need to tolerate and even trust strangers—was first sown, she says.

13 This is one of several hypotheses that Gaydarska and Chapman explore in a new book, *Early Urbanism in Europe*. Perhaps the megasites served a purely ritualistic purpose, being managed by a group of "guardians" who welcomed pilgrims over four or five months of the year—or maybe more intensively, over a single month, in the style of the Burning Man festival held annually in Nevada's Black Rock desert. An alternative idea is that different clans took it in turns to govern, provisioning the site and leading visitors in rituals for a year, before another clan rotated in.

14 By contrast, Müller and his German colleagues believe the megasites were fully occupied all year round. The evidence is fiendishly difficult to interpret, partly because Trypillians periodically burned their houses down in a controlled way—possibly in a deconsecration rite when they moved out. At Nebelivka, where Chapman and Gaydarska work, for instance, two-thirds of the 1,500 houses were torched over its 200 years of existence. Dating techniques don't offer the precision needed to determine what proportion of the houses were inhabited contemporaneously before being burned. The ecological impact of activities at megasites was light, though, as is clear from detailed analyses of pollen, which can indicate cultivation and forest management, and charcoal in sediment cores taken from surrounding land. But whether that was because the sites were only occupied seasonally or because resources were brought in from elsewhere, is unknown.

UNIT **6** Archeology

15 There is another suggestion for why the megasites came to be: Trypillians congregated defensively against some external threat. Here again, the archaeologists disagree. Megasites are typically surrounded by a ditch. The one at Nebelivka is 5 kilometres in circumference. But at 1.5 metres wide and 0.8 metres deep, it would have been easy for an adult to jump, suggesting to the UK-based researchers that it wasn't defensive. However, Videiko says the ditch once contained a palisade—an enclosure made of wooden stakes—that has long since rotted. Either way, there is also protection in numbers.

16 Nikitin also favours the defensive hypothesis. He and David Anthony, an anthropologist at Hartwick College in New York, see the emergence of the megasites as a response to broader regional conflicts. To the south, in what is now Romania and Bulgaria, were the heartlands of Europe's oldest farming cultures. By 4600 BC, these Balkan communities had a flourishing copper industry and were fabulously rich. A gleaming symbol of their wealth is the spectacular, gold- and copper-filled grave of a high-status man discovered at a cemetery in Varna, Bulgaria. Then, around 4200 BC, those farming settlements were abandoned. Archaeologists have found signs of violence just before that happened. Nikitin and Anthony believe the survivors fled north to their distant relations, the Trypillians, and that the megasites, which arose around the same time, were built to accommodate them. "I think these were refugee camps," says Nikitin.

17 If there was a massacre, it isn't clear who was responsible. Was it farmer-on-farmer violence, triggered or exacerbated by the impact of climate fluctuations on harvests? Or did nomads from the steppe to the north and east become aggressive when those farming communities went into decline—perhaps for the same reason—and their copper production dwindled? Finds of Balkan copper deep in the steppe indicate that the two groups had traded for several centuries by then. Although, analyses of individuals from Varna and other Balkan cemeteries suggest that, with rare exceptions, there was no interbreeding.

18 Whatever triggered the slaughter around 4200 BC, the Trypillian farmers further north seem to have been spared—at least to begin with. They continued to interact with nearby steppe people, as evidenced by a type of steppe pottery known as Cucuteni C that crops up in every layer at the megasites until their abandonment. "The Trypillians managed to work it out with the steppe," says Nikitin. And yet they didn't breed with their neighbours either. Nikitin's team found no steppe genes in human remains at a Trypillian site whose occupation overlaps with the megasite period. One reason, he suggests, was their radically different world views. Steppe people valued individual prowess—as demonstrated by their use of coveted Balkan copper to decorate the bodies of their dead chieftains—whereas the essence of Trypillian culture, with its concentric megasites and assembly houses, appears to have been egalitarianism.

19   Unsurprisingly, the refugee camp idea doesn't appeal to everyone. "You can't have a crisis for 800 years that people have not dealt with," says Gaydarska. Others have wondered how relatively small bands of nomads, however warlike, could have destroyed the wealthy, densely populated Balkan farming settlements. Nikitin admits the idea has weak points, not least that building the megasites rapidly, to accommodate migrants, would have required an extraordinarily large investment of labour. Nevertheless, he suggests that it could explain the absence of human remains. "If these were temporary camps, the incomers probably didn't stick around for long and did their dying someplace else," he says.

20   Around 3400 BC, the megasites were abandoned in their turn—though the Trypillians went on, inhabiting smaller, more scattered sites. Anthony thinks that whatever peace the farmers had negotiated with steppe people broke down. Genetic analysis reveals that after the demise of the megasites, the two populations started interbreeding. A tantalising theory that Nikitin is exploring—in collaboration with David Reich's ancient DNA lab at Harvard University—is that the offspring of that genetic mixing were the Yamnaya people. If so, we may need to rewrite the story of these herders, thought to have come from the steppe, who, starting around 5,000 years ago, transformed Europe's population genetically, linguistically and culturally. They have been portrayed as a murderous people, but, perhaps, being already part of European farmers, they were able to complete this transformation peacefully. Though the question remains wide open, Nikitin says it is possible that the Yamnaya came after a violent period and ushered in a new ideology shaped by the steppe. "At the peak of this despair an idea formed, of a new world order," he says.

21   Others think there is no need to invoke outside forces to explain the abandonment of the megasites. Müller, who has excavated principally at a megasite called Maidanetske, says that by 3700 BC, the assembly houses in its quarters and neighbourhoods had gone. Only the largest assembly house remained. "This shows, at least for me, that there was a kind of centralisation of decision-making processes going on," he says. That might have been incompatible with social cohesion. Gaydarska and Chapman also think the problem was internal, noting that as Maidanetske grew, the central space—which could have served a critical function as a gathering place—was filled in. However, another possibility is that the megasites simply lost their prestige, they say. Perhaps, given enough exposure to steppe ideas through trade, the Trypillians began to question their own.

22   In a rare instance of unity, most Trypillian researchers agree that environmental depletion cannot be the reason they left. "It is quite clear that the carrying capacity of this area was never reached," says Müller. They also reject an idea proposed in 2018 by microbiologist Nicolás Rascovan at the Pasteur Institute in Paris and his colleagues. Rascovan argued that plague got a foothold in the megasites, from where it spread north and west, eventually turning up in a Swedish cemetery around 2900 BC. Plague victims' bones would have turned up, says Gaydarska. Moreover, the megasites had been gone for 500 years by then, which is too big a gap even for a relatively slow-moving disease like plague.

23   However it happened, by the time the Yamnaya appeared in Europe, what may have been the world's first urban experiment was over. Far to the south and east, the cities of Egypt and Mesopotamia—built on a radically different model—were thriving, still several centuries off their peak. From then on, civilisation took a new path and the world never looked back. (*New Scientist*, February 27, 2021)

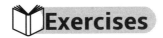

I Fast reading

Task 1 Tick (√) the statement that most closely reflects the writer's point of view.

(　) A. The essence of Trypillian culture seems to have been egalitarianism.

(　) B. The Trypillian megasites were very different from the first cities built centuries later.

(　) C. The Trypillians created the megasites around 6,200 years ago, but the urban experiment finally failed.

(　) D. The Trypillian proto-cities may have been the world's first urban experiment, and they have challenged the ideas about the origins of civilization.

II Annotating skills

Task 2 Read paragraphs 1–10, identify which functions the following paragraphs have, complete the table below using the annotations you have made, and find key information in relevant paragraphs as extra comment.

- background information
- general problem
- solution
- exemplification
- cause
- explication
- implication
- evaluation
- viewpoint
- definition
- transition
- summary
- comparison & contrast
- conclusion

Paragraph(s)	Function	Extra comment
1–3, 6		
4		
5, 7		
8–10		

III Reading for specific information

Task 3 Read Text B carefully, but as fast as you can. Try to answer as many questions as you can without referring to the text.

1. When did the farmers living on the eastern fringes of Europe leave their neolithic villages and move into an area of forest and steppe?

2. Which cities in Mesopotamia are usually considered as the world's first ones?

3. What are the two features considered integral to the definition of a city?

4. Among the several thousand known Trypillian settlements, why are around 15 counted as "mega"?

5. In what way were the megasites laid out?

6. What impact did the activities at megasites have on the ecological environment? How can it be known?

7. According to the text, how many kinds of theories are proposed by scholars to explain why the megasites came to be? What are their main points respectively?

8. According to the finds of Balkan copper deep in the steppe, how long had nomads and farmers in Balkan communities traded when the possible massacre happened? Were they interbred highly?

9. What was the evidence showing that Trypillian farmers were spared in the massacre around 4200 BC?

10. What were the values of steppe people and Trypillian respectively? How are they revealed?

11. Does the refugee idea have any weakness? If it does, can you give an example?

12. When were the megasites abandoned in their turn?

13. According to Anthony, when did steppe people and Trypillians start interbreeding?

14. What is the tantalizing theory explored by Nikitin together with David Reich's ancient DNA lab? If it is true, what could be a new discovery about the history of Yamnaya people?

15. What is the agreement on the reason why the Trypillians abandoned their megasites?

16. How many classes can the theories for the abandonment of the megasites fall into? Can you generalize them?

Task 4 Academic texts often contain quotes from experts within the relevant field. In Text B, the opinions of a number of experts are mentioned. Read the opinions that relate to the two questions below and match each opinion to the relevant expert. The first one has been done for you.

| Mykhailo Videiko | Johannes Müller | John Chapman | Bisserka Gaydarska |
| Monica Smith | Alexey Nikitin | David Anthony | |

Question 1: How should we make sense of them (megasites)?

1. Trypillian sites were basically egalitarian.   John Chapman

2. The megasites as essentially overgrown villages—an experiment, yes, but only in scale.   _____

3. These structural subdivisions might have helped contain disputes, and the assembly houses could have been where decisions were made and communicated.   _____

4. It really was an experiment in social organization—and the appearance of the megasites reflects this ideological shift.   _____

5. The megasites were simply a response to growing population pressure.   _____

Question 2: What were these places (megasites) for? (Why did they congregate?)

1. Megasites were immediate precursors of cities, where people had their first taste of something bigger and more heterogeneous.   Monica Smith

2. Perhaps the megasites served a purely ritualistic purpose, being managed by a group of "guardians" who welcomed pilgrims over four or five months of the year—or maybe more intensively, over a single month.   _____

3. Trypillians congregated defensively against some external threat.   _____

4. The megasites were a response to broader regional conflicts.   _____

5. Megasites were refugee camps.   _____

UNIT **6** Archeology

Task 5 Read the text and try to find the text-referring words in the table. Note down the idea or word(s) that each one refers to. The first one has been done for you.

Text-referring word(s)	Refers to...	Paragraph
This raises another question: What were these places for?	the debate over the numbers of inhabitants	7
This is one of several hypotheses that Gaydarska and Chapman explore in a new book		13
Nikitin also favours *the defensive hypothesis*		16
the *two groups* had traded for several centuries by then		17
he suggests that *it* could explain the absence of human remains.		19
They have been portrayed as a murderous people		20
At the peak of *this despair* an idea formed, of a new world order		20
That might have been incompatible with social cohesion		21

IV Language enhancement

Task 6 Find the word(s) in the text with the same or similar meaning(s) to each of the expressions in the left column of the table below. The first one has been done for you.

Expression	Synonym(s) in text	Paragraph(s)
a place where people have come to live and make their homes	settlement	1
dweller		7

(Continued)

Expression	Synonym(s) in text	Paragraph(s)
just		8
meeting/gathering		10
a thing that comes before something similar and that leads to its development		12
to obey		12
ceremony		12
the killing of a large number of people especially in a cruel way		17, 18
great skill at doing something		18
the belief that all people are equal and should have the same rights and opportunities		18
credit		21
consumption		22

Task 7 Study the words in the table below and identify them in Text B. Write down the possible meaning of each one in context.

Word	Possible meaning	Paragraph
concentrically	with a common center	7
quarter		10
subdivide		10
pilgrimage		12
external		15
accommodate		16
breed		18
incompatible		21
plague		22

UNIT 6 Archeology

V Reading skills: Reading actively

Task 8 One way to read actively is to respond to the cues that the writer provides to follow the argument in the text. As you read Text B, use the cues to ask questions as the table below has shown.

Cue	Question(s)
one reason, purpose, function, suggestion	What is the second, third, etc., reason, function, purpose?
there are *other* reasons, functions, uses	What are they? Did the writer already name one?
in some cases, X happens	What happens in other cases?
as a *result*	What was the cause? Did I miss that?
not only	What else? Who else?
there are *two/three/several...* reasons/types	What are they? Did the writer number them?
finally	What were the first one and the second? Did I miss them?
some/others think/believe/view...	What do some/others think/believe/view...?
this (raises...) *another* question:	What is the "one question"?
there is *another* (suggestion...)	What is the "one suggestion"?

Task 9 Find at least three examples with these cues in Text B. Find the answer in the text and highlight it. Try to ask questions that go with each cue.

1. Cue: _____ Para. (7)
   The answer to the question going with the cue: _____ Para. (   )
2. Cue: _____ Para. (15)
   The answer to the question going with the cue: _____ Para. (   )
3. Cue: _____ Para. (8)
   The answer to the question going with the cue: _____ Para. (   )
   _____ Para. (   )

143

UNIT 7

Science of Health

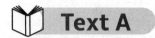

Text A

Running or Walking

1. I hated physical education at school. Cross-country was the worst: cold, boring and lung-burning. "Run, don't walk!" the teacher would shout as we jogged reluctantly through the mud, only to walk as soon as we were out of sight.

2. Over the following four decades, my PE teacher's angry barks have been echoed in the constant media reports telling me that I should run, whether informing me that jogging could increase my lifespan by years or that training for a marathon would make my heart younger.

3. The benefits of exercise are huge. If it were a drug, it would be a miracle cure. It keeps our hearts strong and blood vessels supple, lessens chronic inflammation and reduces the harmful effects of stress.

4. But do we need to run to get the benefits or can we get a sufficient dose just from walking in the limited time we have for exercise? And what about those who warn about the toll on joints from pounding the pavement? It is common knowledge that running causes arthritis and ruins the knees and hips—but does the evidence back this up? I wanted to find out if my PE teacher's mantra was right.

5. The idea that running is the best exercise for us—indeed, that it is part of what makes us human—has many champions. Among them is Daniel Lieberman at Harvard University, who maintains that we evolved to run long distances. He thinks that our now largely untapped talent for persistence hunting—chasing animals over long distances—in hot conditions gives us an edge over other animals and shaped our evolutionary history.

6. And we aren't just good at running because we are good at walking—in fact, technically they are quite different. A range of adaptations such as sweat glands and hairless skin to aid cooling, the right balance of muscle types and a special ligament to keep our head stable when running all mean that, over long distances, we can outrun almost any other animal. "Thanks to our evolutionary history, all of us have the anatomy and physiology needed to walk and run—assuming we are not disabled," says Lieberman. "In today's world, we have medicalised, commodified and commercialised exercise, but physical activity, at its heart, is something we evolved to do."

UNIT **7** Science of Health

⟨7⟩ It is somewhat ironic then that many of us today are almost entirely sedentary. The current U.S. and U.K. government guidelines for physical activity recommend that adults do at least 2.5 hours of moderate exercise or 75 minutes of vigorous exercise every week. In the U.S., only half the population meet these guidelines, and the situation is only slightly better in the U.K. But what counts as moderate and vigorous exercise?

⟨8⟩ Back in the late 1980s, Bill Haskell at Stanford University in California asked the same question and came up with a benchmark to compare exercise against sitting quietly. When seated, we expend about 1 kilocalorie per hour for each kilogram of body mass. Haskell and his colleagues called this a metabolic equivalent, or 1 MET. For an 80-kilogram person, this resting metabolic rate represents around 1,920 kcals per day.

Taking It Easy

⟨9⟩ All physical activities can be expressed in METs, and there is now a Compendium of Physical Activities that contains an eclectic mix of them described using this system. This elegant solution to the definition of exercise has three categories: light exercise up to 3 METs, moderate exercise between 3 and 6 METs and vigorous exercise for anything over 6 METs (see Figure 7-1).

The energy expended during exercise can be measured in metabolic equivalents (METs), where 1 MET is the metabolic rate at rest. Walking counts as vigorous exercise, if you go fast enough.

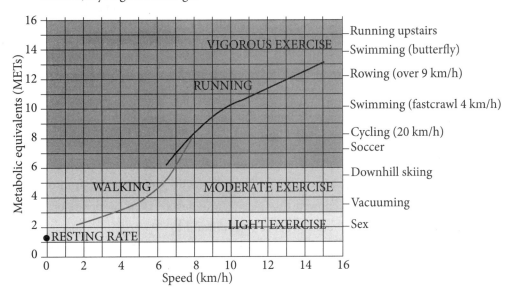

Source: Compendium of Physical Activities

Figure 7-1 Measuring the Burn

10 Strolling, at about 2 METs, is light exercise, while walking briskly is in the middle of moderate at 5 METs. The transition to running at around 7 kilometres per hour is where exercise enters the vigorous category. A really brisk walk and a slow run are roughly the same, in terms of effort and calories burned. But is this true of their health benefits too?

11 At first glance, it might seem that running has the upper hand here. A study from January, for example, was enough to make anyone sign up for a marathon. This looked at 138 first-time marathon runners and found that training for and completing the 26-mile race, even at a slow pace, is equivalent to a 4-year reduction in age of the cardiovascular system, or even more for those who are older and less fit.

12 Running also gets a glowing bill of health in several large-scale studies that follow people for many years: They show that this exercise has a dose-related effect. More running is better, though with diminishing returns, but the good news for couch potatoes is that the largest gains come by going from nothing to something. "The biggest health benefits are observed with just a little running per week, less than 60 minutes, an amount that would fit in most people's schedules," says Angelique Brellenthin, an exercise researcher at Iowa State University.

13 Further benefits are clear from long-term U.S. studies. In the National Walkers' and National Runners' health studies, Paul Williams and Paul Thompson of the Lawrence Berkeley National Laboratory measured the health of about 16,000 walkers and 33,000 runners over six years. Compared with walkers, runners had a 38 percent lower risk of high blood pressure and a 71 percent lower risk of type 2 diabetes.

14 When the researchers controlled energy expenditure and weight difference between the groups, however, the benefits from walking and running were comparable. Williams later analysed data for breast and brain cancer, and the reductions in risk of death from running or walking were, again, similar if energy expenditure was the same.

15 Even a small amount of exercise brings significant health gains. This was the case in a massive study from 2011 that followed more than 400,000 people in Taiwan, China over an average of eight years, noting their exercise habits and the number of deaths from different causes. This showed that just 15 minutes a day of moderate exercise such as fast walking was enough to reduce risk of death by 10 percent compared with sedentary participants. This effect could also be gained by around 5 minutes of vigorous exercise such as running, giving a time-versus-benefit ratio between running and walking of three to one (see Figure 7-2).

Even a small amount of exercise boosts health, but this effect tapers off with increasing time spent exercising.

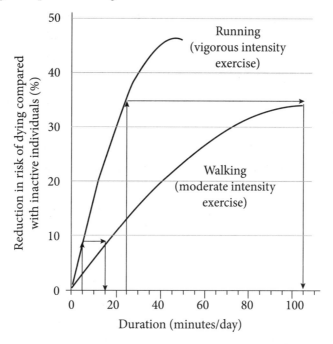

A 5-minute run generates the same benefits as a 15-minute walk, and a 25-minute run is equivalent to a 105-minute walk.

Figure 7-2   Survival of the Fittest

16   So far, so clear. If you have time on your hands, the gains of walking are comparable to those of a jog so long as you are moving at a moderate pace. But for the time poor, running is the best way to get a dose of exercise. "The fact that running confers similar benefits as walking but in half the time is one major reason that running is attractive for health," says Brellenthin. "There may be additional benefits of running, particularly for cardiovascular health, related to the higher intensity of running. However, intensity is relative to individual fitness levels, and a brisk walk will provide numerous health benefits for people like beginners and older adults."

17   This is great news for joggers and hikers, but not if our body gets worn out or injured in the process. Could this risk outweigh the benefits?

18   There is no doubt that running is a high-impact activity. When the foot hits the ground, a force equivalent to two or three times your body weight pushes up through the body. Bones, joints, muscles and ligaments must absorb this force. The question is whether this wears your joints out, as many of us believe.

19   As I get older, this is something I worry about. I'm not alone. "Most people understand that exercise is good for you, that it is good for the cardiovascular system, but at what expense, if you've worn your knees out in the process?" says Alister Hart, a surgeon at the Royal National Orthopaedic Hospital in London. This question was on his mind back in 2012, when he was hobbling around after completing his first marathon, so he decided to study the impact of marathon running on knees.

20   Together with his colleague Laura Maria Horga and others, he recruited 82 runners taking part in the London marathon, all of whom were over 40 and had never run this distance before. Using MRI, the runners' knees were scanned in detail six months before the race and again a few weeks after. The scans revealed that the knee's main weight-bearing compartments—the parts most likely to develop arthritis in the long term—had become stronger as a result of the marathon training. "It was a very big surprise," says Hart.

21   The kneecap part of the joint, however, did show damage, but follow-up scans revealed that this had reversed six months later, when the participants had reverted to less intense running regimes. Hart's take-home message is "distance running can have long-term benefits for your knees". The team also did a study on hips, which found that 560 kilometres of a marathon training programme, ending in the race, didn't cause pre-arthritic changes in the hip joint. "Our findings suggest that the high impact forces during marathon running were well tolerated by the hip joint," says Horga.

Wear and Tear

22   Another treasure trove of data on wear and tear comes from the National Walkers' and National Runners' health studies. As part of this, Williams looked at osteoarthritis, which is caused by the breakdown of bones or cartilage in joints. He found that doing more running or walking actually reduced the risk of osteoarthritis and the need for hip replacements. It didn't seem to matter if the participants walked briskly or ran slowly.

23   The idea that running wears the body out is a myth, says Lieberman. "In fact, quite the reverse. Running helps activate all kinds of repair and maintenance mechanisms," he says.

24   But it is possible to overdo it. A 2017 meta-analysis including more than 125,000 people found that 3.5 percent of recreational runners had osteoarthritis in the hip or knee compared with 10 percent of sedentary non-runners. Yet 13 percent of elite runners who had taken part in international competitions had such osteoarthritis. For recreational runners at least, it seems there is a sweet spot at which running protects against osteoarthritis.

25   That is good news for most joggers, but what about the risk of strains and sprains? "Running, like everything, however, has trade-offs including greater risk of injury," says Lieberman.

26   When it comes to injuries such as sprains, walking beats running hands down. A study of the exercise habits of more than 14,000 Spanish graduates, for instance, found walking resulted in 40 percent fewer injuries than running for equal energy expended. The injury rate of running was less than that of football, sailing and martial arts, and similar to that of skiing and tennis.

27   The risk of injuries from running depends on factors such as how long you have been doing it, as well as your age and sex. A 2015 meta-analysis of 13 studies of running-related injuries found that novice runners were most likely to get injured, sustaining around 18 injuries per 1,000 hours of exercise. At an average pace of nearly 10 kilometres per hour, this is equivalent to about one injury every 540 kilometres, more than double the rate of more experienced runners. Unsurprisingly, one of the most important risks is the existence of a previous injury. "I think learning how to run sensibly and properly can help mitigate those risks," says Lieberman.

Weighty Issue

28   But what about those terrifying stories of people who cross a marathon finish line only to drop dead? Some studies show that the health benefits of running tail off, or even reverse, when running more than 4.5 hours a week. Crucially though, the risks from any amount of running are always lower than from doing no running at all and, on average, runners live three years longer than non-runners. "People who engage in high amounts of running still have health benefits compared to non-runners, but there is probably a point of diminishing returns," says Brellenthin.

29   There is good news for runners on the obesity front too: Runners tend to weigh less than walkers. This could be because thinner people are more likely to run, but a study by Williams suggests running helps shed excess weight. It showed that reductions in body mass index were significantly greater from running compared with walking when these activities were matched for energy expenditure. This could be due to a greater increase in metabolic rate after more intense exercise.

30   So where does this leave us in the walk/run debate? Was my PE teacher right that running is a better way to exercise than walking?

31   The research clearly shows that both are good for you. They improve cardiorespiratory fitness and reduce blood pressure, body mass index and the risk of a host of diseases. For the biggest bang for your buck though, running has the edge,

mostly because you can get more exercise done in a given time. But if you expend the same amount of energy when you walk, the benefits are quite similar. In other words, if you prefer walking, go for a long one, ideally with a few hills. And remember that any amount of exercise is better than none.

32   This philosophy might explain the success of an exercise phenomenon that is sweeping the globe: parkrun. These free, timed 5-kilometre community events take place every Saturday morning in more than 20 countries. They are wildly popular, with 6 million people signed up. Key to parkrun's success is that you can cover the distance however you want: by running, walking, pushing a child in a buggy or loping with a dog. Participants rate the impact on their fitness and happiness so highly (I know, because I carried out the research to find out) that family doctors in the U.K. now prescribe parkrun to their patients.

33   My PE teacher would be astonished to discover that I enjoy running now and rarely miss a parkrun. If I did meet him, though, I would gently point out that we don't necessarily have to run. After all, the most important exercise is the one you actually do. (*New Scientist*, March 14, 2020)

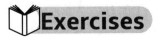
Exercises

I Fast reading

Task 1 Tick (√) the statement that most closely reflects the writer's point of view.

(   ) A. Walking beats running hands down in terms of injuries.

(   ) B. Running can make participants gain bigger health benefits than walking, such as reduction in age of the cardiovascular system, chronic inflammation and the harmful effects of stress.

(   ) C. Walking and running are roughly the same in terms of effort and calories burned.

(   ) D. Benefits of walking and running are comparable when energy expenditure and weight difference are controlled.

UNIT **7** Science of Health

II Annotating skills

Task 2 Identify which functions the following paragraphs of the text have, complete the table below using the annotations you have made, and find key information in relevant paragraphs as extra comment. The first one has been done for you.

- background information
- general problem
- solution
- exemplification
- cause
- explication
- implication
- evaluation
- viewpoint
- definition
- transition
- summary
- comparison & contrast
- conclusion

Paragraph(s)	Function	Extra comment
1–2	background information	introducing the topic with personal experience
3		
4		
5–6		
7		
8–10		
11–16		
17		
18–25		
26		
27		
28		
29		
30–33		

153

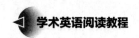

III Reading for specific information

Task 3 Read Text A carefully, but as fast as you can. Try to answer as many questions as you can without referring to the text.

1. Why did the writer hate physical education at school?

2. What are the benefits of running according to the media reports?

3. What are the benefits of exercise according to the writer?

4. Who maintains that we evolved to run long distances?

5. Can humans outrun any other animals over long distances?

6. How long do people need to do physical activity according to the U.S. and U.K. government guidelines?

7. What are the three categories of exercise according to Compendium of Physical Activities?

8. How can we do exercise to reduce risk of death by 10 percent?

9. Who are suitable for a brisk walk?

10. According to Williams, how does running affect osteoarthritis and the need for hip replacements?

11. Which factors will influence the risk of injuries from running?

12. Why are reductions in body mass index greater from running when running and walking are matched for energy expenditure?

Task 4 Read the text and try to find the text-referring words in the table. Note down the idea or word(s) that each one refers to. The first one has been done for you.

Text-referring word(s)	Refers to...	Paragraph
Bill Haskell at Stanford University in California asked *the same question*	what counts as moderate and vigorous exercise?	8

UNIT **7** Science of Health

(Continued)

Text-referring word(s)	Refers to...	Paragraph
But is *this* true of their health benefits too		10
This was the case in a massive study from 2011		15
This is great news for joggers and hikers		17
The question is whether *this* wears your joints out		18
That is good news for most joggers		25
But what about *those terrifying stories* of people		28
This could be because thinner people are more likely to run		29
This philosophy might explain the success of an exercise phenomenon that is sweeping the globe		32

IV Language enhancement

Task 5 Locate the phrases in the text and complete the table below by explaining the meaning of each italicized word in your own words. Pay attention to the writer's choice of the adjective or adverb for emphasis. The first one has been done for you.

Phrase	Meaning	Paragraph
constant media reports	happening all the time	2
miracle cure		3
sufficient dose		4
untapped talent		5
entirely sedentary		7
eclectic mix		9
vigorous exercise		9
significant health gains		15
massive study		15

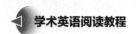

(Continued)

Phrase	Meaning	Paragraph
additional benefits		16
high-impact activity		18
novice runners		27

Task 6 Locate the phrases in the text and try to work out their meanings in context. Think about how the writer uses the phrases below and the effect the writer's use of language has on the reader. The first one has been done for you.

Phrase	Meaning	Paragraph
pound the pavement	to walk or run on the street	4
back... up		4
the upper hand		11
a glowing bill of		12
a dose of		16
worn out		17
on one's mind		19
hobble around		19
take-home message		21
a sweet spot		24
trade-off		25
beat hands down		26
tail off		28
a host of		31
the biggest bang for your buck		31

UNIT 7 Science of Health

V Reading skills: Examining graphics

Task 7 Displayed information such as artworks, tables of data, bar, pie and flow charts, maps, photographs and timelines are often referred to as graphics. Study Figure 7-1 in the text. What do you understand through the terms listed?

1. the burn: _____

2. metabolic rate: _____

3. vigorous exercise: _____

4. vacuuming: _____

Task 8 Answer the following questions relating to Figure 7-1.

1. What is Figure 7-1 about?

2. How much energy expended is regarded as light exercise?

3. What types of exercise are taken as moderate ones?

4. Which type of exercise is the most vigorous one in terms of METs?

5. How much energy expended during walking is considered as vigorous exercise?

Task 9 Summarize the most significant data that Figure 7-1 displays. Write no more than two sentences.

_____

_____.

Text B

Rethinking Mental Health

Dan Jones

1. Life can be tough. All of us have experienced nagging worries, anxiety, sadness, low mood and paranoid thoughts. Most of the time this is short-lived. But when it persists or worsens, our lives can quickly unravel.

2. Mental health conditions, including everything from depression and phobias to anorexia and schizophrenia, are shockingly common. In the U.K., one in four people experience them each year, so it is likely that you, or someone you know, has sought help from a professional. That process usually begins with a diagnosis—a mental health professional evaluates your symptoms and determines which of the hundreds of conditions listed in psychiatry's classification bible, the *Diagnostic and Statistical Manual of Mental Disorders*, best fits. Then you start on a treatment tailored to your condition. It seems an obvious approach, but is it the right one? "For millennia, we've put all these psychiatric conditions in separate corners," says neuroscientist Anke Hammerschlag at Vrije University Amsterdam, the Netherlands. "But maybe that's not how it works biologically."

3. There is growing and compelling evidence that she is correct. Instead of being separate conditions, many mental health problems appear to share an underlying cause, something researchers now call the "p factor". This realisation could radically change how we diagnose and treat mental health conditions, putting more focus on symptoms instead of labels and offering more general treatments. It also explains puzzling patterns in the occurrence of these conditions in individuals and families. Rethinking mental health this way could be revolutionary: "I don't think there are such things as [discrete] mental disorders," says behavioural geneticist Robert Plomin at King's College London. "They're just fictions we create because of the medical model."

4. At first glance, the idea that different mental health conditions with distinct symptoms share an underlying cause seems counter-intuitive. The key to understanding it lies in its name. "p factor" has intentional parallels with one of the most famous concepts in psychology. More than a century ago, British psychologist Charles Spearman noted that children's performance on one kind of mental task, say verbal fluency, was correlated with their mental skill in other areas, like mathematical reasoning, spatial

manipulation and logic. In other words, children who are good at one thing tend to be good at another, while those who struggle in one area tend to struggle in others. Using a statistical tool called factor analysis, Spearman showed that this is because these different mental abilities are all linked to an overarching cognitive capacity, which he named general intelligence, or the g factor.

5 A century on, applying the same approach to mental health diagnoses provided the first hints that something similar might be going on. There are a wide range of mental health conditions that manifest with different behavioural and psychological symptoms. Like cognitive skills, they cluster together in individuals, either at the same time or one after another. In 2012, Benjamin Lahey at the University of Chicago and his colleagues analysed information on such diagnoses among 30,000 people studied over three years. Using factor analysis, they found that the observed patterns of illness were best explained by a general tendency towards mental health conditions.

6 The following year, Avshalom Caspi and Terrie Moffitt at King's College London got the same result. Their study used information from 1,000 people whose health had been tracked for four decades since their birth in the early 1970s. It was Moffitt and Caspi who coined the term "p factor" to describe an individual's broad susceptibility to mental health problems. "Once you have any given mental disorder, it increases the likelihood that you'll have multiple other kinds of disorders," says Caspi.

Puzzling Heritability

7 The p factor can also explain puzzling patterns of mental health conditions within families. It had long been known that these conditions have a genetic basis, and are highly heritable. Huge twin studies have estimated the heritability of schizophrenia, for example, at nearly 80 percent, and major depression at about 45 percent. But having a parent or sibling diagnosed with a given condition doesn't just increase the odds that you will experience it. It also increases the likelihood that you will be diagnosed with a different condition. For instance, if a parent has schizophrenia, your risk of developing bipolar disorder doubles, and vice versa. That makes sense if you inherit not just a risk for one kind of condition, but a more generalised risk: the p factor.

8 Indeed, the application of genetics to psychiatry in the past decade has provided key support for the existence of the p factor. In the early days, psychiatric genetics mostly entailed a hunt for individual genes conferring significant risk for developing certain conditions. But this so-called candidate gene approach hit the skids. "It was really a dead loss, but it was all we could do at the time," says Plomin. "Then SNP chips came along in the mid-2000s and changed everything."

9   SNP (single-nucleotide polymorphism, pronounced "snip") chips, which look a bit like the memory card in a digital camera, allow scientists to use a small DNA sample to scan someone's genome and discover which genetic variants they carry. Everyone has millions of single-letter differences in DNA's four-letter code: where one person has a T, for example, another might have a G (and someone else could have A or C). More than 10 million of these SNPs have been identified, and a single SNP chip can detect a million or more of them in one go.

10   The breakthrough for the p factor idea came a few years before Moffitt and Caspi coined the term. In 2009, the International Schizophrenia Consortium used SNP chips to genetically analyse more than 3,000 people diagnosed with the condition. Instead of pulling out one or a few genetic variants with big impacts on schizophrenia susceptibility, the analysis found the condition was linked to thousands of variants, each having a small effect. Intriguingly, these same variants also increased the risk of bipolar disorder.

Shared Genes

11   Later, this kind of analysis was extended. In 2013, an international group called the Psychiatric Genomics Consortium completed a landmark study. Scientists analysed genomic data from more than 30,000 people diagnosed with conditions including bipolar disorder, major depression or schizophrenia. Again, genetic risk variants cut across the traditional diagnostic boundaries of psychiatry. "It's the opposite of what was expected," says Mike Gandal at the University of California, Los Angeles. "Until recently, it was thought that genetic studies would reveal more biological specificity for each disorder, but instead we're seeing all this shared genetics."

12   Tellingly, the story is very different for neurological conditions, which affect the nervous system itself, such as Alzheimer's, Parkinson's, Huntington's and multiple sclerosis. A 2018 study from the Brainstorm Consortium based at Harvard University examined genetic data from more than 265,000 people with one of 25 psychiatric and neurological conditions. This revealed that neurological conditions have little or nothing genetically in common with each other or with psychiatric conditions, making them a much better fit for the classical medical model.

13   For neurological conditions in which single genes play a big role, people can be divided into two groups: those who carry the risk variant and those who don't. The picture is much messier for mental health conditions. The thousands of SNPs underlying them follow a bell-shaped distribution, meaning that a small percentage of people have very few risk variants, a small percentage have a lot, and most people fall somewhere in

between, with symptom severity roughly tracking this curve. "There's no break point at which the number of variants suddenly leads to a diagnosable psychiatric disorder," says Plomin.

14   It gets messier. Researchers are now discovering some SNPs associated with individual conditions. "There's this huge genetic overlap between psychiatric disorders, but there are also some specific genetic factors that make people differ in their symptoms," says Christel Middeldorp, who studies psychiatric genetics at the University of Queensland, Australia. "The p factor doesn't explain everything."

15   In addition, as Caspi is quick to stress, there is more to the story than genes. "The genetic work is exciting, but what's really remarkable about most psychiatric disorders is that they share the same environmental and psychosocial risk factors as well," he says. "Child abuse of any kind, for example, predicts every condition under the sun." The same is true for drug and alcohol abuse, and traumatic experiences during childhood such as being displaced by warfare.

16   Plomin and his colleagues recently attempted to quantify the genetic component of the p factor. Drawing on information from more than 7,000 pairs of twins, they estimated its heritability at around 55 percent. This means that genetic differences explain just over half of the variation between people's general susceptibility to mental health problems, with the rest being driven by non-genetic factors. The study also showed that the p factor is stable across a person's lifetime.

17   Despite these complications, there is growing recognition that mental health conditions have a shared genetic basis, and the search is on to find out how this manifests biologically. In 2018, Gandal and his colleague Dan Geschwind led a team to do just that. They analysed gene expression in the cerebral cortex—the brain's outer layer where higher cognition occurs—from 700 post-mortems of people diagnosed with mental health conditions. "We found that disorders that share the most genetic risk factors, like schizophrenia and bipolar disorder, look very similar in the gene-expression patterns as well," says Gandal. Many of the genes involved controlled activity at synapses, the junctions between neurons.

18   A recent study led by Hammerschlag backs this up. Her team investigated more than 7,000 sets of genes involved in a wide range of biological pathways, and then looked at which contained genes with variants linked to five common mental health conditions. Only 14 fit the bill. "Almost all of these gene sets have a function in neurons, and most play a role in the synapse," she says. In other words, the p factor seems to have something to do with communication between brain cells.

19 The latest research is even more enlightening. Maxime Taquet at the University of Oxford and his colleagues believe they have identified a "vulnerability network" in the brains of children at high genetic risk of developing mental health conditions. Comparing their brain scans with those of children with a low genetic susceptibility, the team found large differences in three key areas: a structure called the default network that is active while the brain is at rest, a second structure involved in planning and control, and the part of the brain that processes vision. In a similar study, Caspi and Moffitt found that people with a higher p factor have differences in a brain circuit crucial for monitoring and processing information so it can be used in higher cortical functions such as regulating emotions, thoughts and behaviours.

20 It is still something of a mystery how having a brain with these sorts of features might influence an individual's psychology. Caspi and Mofftt think that a high p factor probably manifests as a combination of disordered thinking, difficulties regulating emotions and a tendency towards negative feelings. However, even if these links aren't yet clear, the p factor idea may be useful for diagnosing and treating mental health conditions.

21 Already, many drugs are known to be beneficial in supposedly distinct diagnoses. "In practice, we often use the same treatment for different disorders," says psychiatrist Tova Fuller at the University of California, San Francisco. "Antipsychotics, for example, are useful not only in psychosis, but also in mania, delirium, agitation and other conditions." The p factor makes sense of these "transdiagnostic" therapies. Yet they weren't developed with it in mind. "If we can figure out the biology of the p factor, then it might be possible to target the mechanisms involved and develop therapies that work better across disorders," says Gandal. "These could be given to a large number of patients, rather than treating each person based on their specific pattern of symptoms."

22 Talk-based treatments, such as cognitive behavioural therapy (CBT), also have transdiagnostic value. "There are always lessons for the patient on how to reframe stressful experiences and look on the bright side, how to identify triggers that set off their symptoms, and guidance on life skills," says Moffitt. Currently, there are separate therapeutic guidelines for specific conditions. However, the p factor idea lends support to clinicians advocating a one-size-fits-all version of CBT called the common elements treatment approach in an attempt to ensure that more people globally get the treatment they need. "It's a front-line cognitive therapy that can be offered to everybody who has mental distress," says Moffitt. "Then, after that, people could be referred onwards to a specialist who treats, say, only schizophrenia or panic attacks, depending on the symptoms present."

23   Moffitt also believes that the existence of the p factor should prompt a shift from treating conditions themselves to treating the often distressing symptoms people experience. "We tend to think: This person has depression today, so this is a person who is depressive and we really need to focus on depression," she says. "We obviously need to treat their depressive symptoms, but, knowing that this patient will present with different symptoms in the future, we also need to provide them with tools and skills to cope when they arise."

24   Plomin goes even further. For him, the blurred biological lines between mental health conditions alongside the genetic continuity of susceptibility across populations demolish the orthodox view of mental illness. "I think these diagnostic classifications are mostly a myth," he says. That doesn't mean people don't experience mental health problems that require the help of a professional, but Plomin would be happy to see the current model of psychiatry go the way of the dodo. "It's caused a lot of harm because it implies there are mentally ill people versus 'normals'," he says. "Really we're all somewhere along a continuum." (*New Scientist*, January 25, 2020)

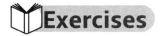

I Fast reading

Task 1 Tick (√) the statement that most closely reflects the writer's point of view.

(   ) A. Mental health conditions, such as depression, phobias, anorexia and schizophrenia are common.

(   ) B. Many mental health conditions within families have a genetic basis and are highly heritable.

(   ) C. Neurological conditions have little in common with each other genetically.

(   ) D. Growing evidence that many mental health conditions share an underlying cause could transform their treatment.

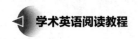

II Annotating skills

Task 2 Look at the example of annotations below and complete the following table with the annotations you have made.

- background information
- exemplification
- implication
- definition
- comparison & contrast
- general problem
- cause
- evaluation
- transition
- conclusion
- solution
- explication
- viewpoint
- summary

Example:

Annotations	Text extract from Paragraph 3
transition viewpoint implication evaluation explication	There is growing and compelling evidence that she is correct. Instead of being separate conditions, many mental health problems appear to share an underlying cause, something researchers now call the "p factor". This realisation could radically change how we diagnose and treat mental health conditions, putting more focus on symptoms instead of labels and offering more general treatments. It also explains puzzling patterns in the occurrence of these conditions in individuals and families. Rethinking mental health this way could be revolutionary: "I don't think there are such things as [discrete] mental disorders," says behavioural geneticist Robert Plomin at King's College London. "They're just fictions we create because of the medical model."

Annotations	Text extract from Paragraph 7
_____ _____ _____ _____	The p factor can also explain puzzling patterns of mental health conditions within families. It had long been known that these conditions have a genetic basis, and are highly heritable. Huge twin studies have estimated the heritability of schizophrenia, for example, at nearly 80 percent, and major depression at about 45 percent. But having a parent

(Continued)

Annotations	Text extract from Paragraph 7
_____ _____	or sibling diagnosed with a given condition doesn't just increase the odds that you will experience it. It also increases the likelihood that you will be diagnosed with a different condition. For instance, if a parent has schizophrenia, your risk of developing bipolar disorder doubles, and vice versa. That makes sense if you inherit not just a risk for one kind of condition, but a more generalised risk: the p factor.

III Reading for specific information

Task 3 Read Text B carefully, but as fast as you can. Try to answer as many questions as you can without referring to the text.

1. How many people experience mental health conditions each year in the U.K.?

2. What is the underlying cause of many mental health problems?

3. How important is the "p factor"?

4. What is "g factor"?

5. What are the similarities between cognitive skills and mental health conditions?

6. Who was the first one to create the term "p factor"?

7. What can be implied from huge twin studies?

8. What is the key support for the existence of the p factor?

9. What are the functions of SNP chips?

10. What did the landmark study reveal?

11. What makes neurological conditions a much better fit for the classical medical model?

12. What is really remarkable about most psychiatric disorders?

13. What is the percentage of genetic component in the p factor?

14. What did Taquet and his colleagues at the University of Oxford find?

15. How do Caspi and Moffit think of the high p factor according to Paragraph 20?

Task 4 Academic texts often contain quotes from experts within the relevant field. In Text B, the opinions of a number of experts are mentioned. Read the opinions below. Then scan the text for information, matching each opinion to the relevant expert. The first one has been done for you.

| Anke Hammerschlag | Avshalom Caspi | Mike Gandal |
| Robert Plomin | Christel Middeldorp | Terrie Moffitt |

1. Until recently, it was thought that genetic studies would reveal more biological specificity for each disorder, but instead we're seeing all this shared genetics. __Mike Gandal__

2. There's this huge genetic overlap between psychiatric disorders, but there are also some specific genetic factors that make people differ in their symptoms. _____

3. For millennia, we've put all these psychiatric conditions in separate corners, but maybe that's not how it works biologically. _____

4. There's no break point at which the number of variants suddenly leads to a diagnosable psychiatric disorder. _____

5. Almost all of these gene sets have a function in neurons, and most play a role in the synapse. _____

6. Once you have any given mental disorder, it increases the likelihood that you'll have multiple other kinds of disorders. _____

7. We obviously need to treat their depressive symptoms, but, knowing that this patient will present with different symptoms in the future, we also need to provide them with tools and skills to cope when they arise. _____

8. The genetic work is exciting, but what's really remarkable about most psychiatric disorders is that they share the same environmental and psychosocial risk factors as well. _____

UNIT 7 Science of Health

IV Language enhancement

Task 5 Locate the words in the text. Try to work out their meanings in academic context and identify their word class. The first one has been done for you.

Word	Meaning in academic context	Word class	Paragraph
short-lived	not lasting long	adjective	1
professional			2
revolutionary			3
reason			4
manifest			5
cluster			5
coin			6
odds			7
hunt			8
confer			8
intriguingly			10
tellingly			12
fit			12
quantify			16
function			18
circuit			19
supposedly			21
target			21
prompt			23
demolish			24
versus			24
somewhere			24

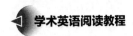

Task 6 Locate the words or phrases in the text and try to work out their meanings in context. Think about how the writer uses the words or phrases below and the effect the writer's choice of language has on the reader. The first one has been done for you.

Word or phrase	Meaning	Paragraph
hit the skids	to decrease in value or status	8
a dead loss		8
in one go		9
pull out		10
cut across		11
under the sun		15
fit the bill		18
make sense		21
figure out		21
set off		22
one-size-fits-all		22
front-line		22
go the way of the dodo		24

V Reading skills: Cohesion and coherence

Task 7 Find examples of cohesion and coherence in Text B and complete the flow chart below. You may use some of the information in the flow chart to write the first draft of your summary.

Example 1

Topic: Mental health

Para 1. All of us have experienced 1) _____.

Para 2. 2) _____ are common… we've put 3) _____ in separate corners, but that's not how it works 4) _____.

Para 3. 5) _____ appear to share an underlying cause: 6) _____.

UNIT 7 Science of Health

Example 2

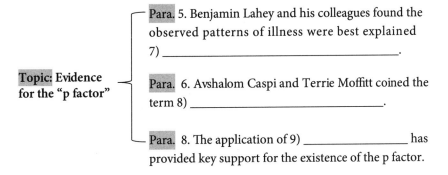

Topic: Evidence for the "p factor"

Para. 5. Benjamin Lahey and his colleagues found the observed patterns of illness were best explained 7) _____.

Para. 6. Avshalom Caspi and Terrie Moffitt coined the term 8) _____.

Para. 8. The application of 9) _____ has provided key support for the existence of the p factor.

Example 3

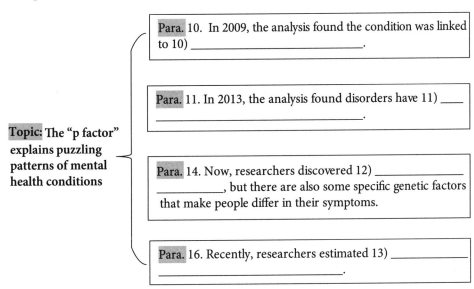

Topic: The "p factor" explains puzzling patterns of mental health conditions

Para. 10. In 2009, the analysis found the condition was linked to 10) _____.

Para. 11. In 2013, the analysis found disorders have 11) _____.

Para. 14. Now, researchers discovered 12) _____, but there are also some specific genetic factors that make people differ in their symptoms.

Para. 16. Recently, researchers estimated 13) _____.

169

UNIT 8

Environment and Climate

Text A

First, Protect Today's Forests

Susan Milius

① Between a death and a burial was hardly the best time to show up in a remote village in Madagascar to make a pitch for forest protection. Bad timing, however, turned out to be the easy problem.

② This forest was the first one that botanist Armand Randrianasolo had tried to protect. He's the first native of Madagascar to become a Ph.D. taxonomist at Missouri Botanical Garden, or MBG, in St. Louis. So he was picked to join a 2002 scouting trip to choose a conservation site.

③ Other groups had already come into the country and protected swaths of green, focusing on "big forests; big, big, big!" Randrianasolo says. Preferably forests with lots of big-eyed, fluffy lemurs to tug heartstrings elsewhere in the world.

④ The Missouri group, however, planned to go small and to focus on the island's plants, legendary among botanists but less likely to be loved as a stuffed cuddly. The team zeroed in on fragments of humid forest that thrive on sand along the eastern coast. "Nobody was working on it," he says.

⑤ As the people of the Agnalazaha forest were mourning a member of their close-knit community, Randrianasolo decided to pay his respects: "I wanted to show that I'm still Malagasy," he says. He had grown up in a seaside community to the north.

⑥ The village was filling up with visiting relatives and acquaintances, a great chance to talk with many people in the region. The deputy mayor conceded that after a morning visit to the bereaved, Randrianasolo and MBG's Chris Birkinshaw could speak in the afternoon with anyone wishing together at the roofed marketplace.

⑦ The two scientists didn't get the reception they'd hoped for. Their pitch to help the villagers conserve their forest while still serving people's needs met protests from the crowd: "You're lying!"

⑧ The community was still upset about a different forest that outside conservationists had protected. The villagers had assumed they would still be able to take trees for lumber, harvest their medicinal plants or sell other bits from the forest during cash emergencies. They were wrong. That place was now off-limits. People caught doing any of the normal things a forest community does would be considered poachers. When

MBG proposed conserving yet more land, residents weren't about to get tricked again. "This is the only forest we have left," they told the scientists.

9 Finding some way out of such clashes to save existing forests has become crucial for fighting climate change. Between 2001 and 2019, the planet's forests trapped an estimated 7.6 billion metric tons of carbon dioxide a year, an international team reported in *Nature Climate Change* in March. That rough accounting suggests trees may capture about one and a half times the annual emissions of the United States, one of the largest global emitters.

10 Planting trees by the millions and trillions is basking in round-the-world enthusiasm right now. Yet saving the forests we already have ranks higher in priority and in payoff, say a variety of scientists.

11 How to preserve forests may be a harder question than why. Success takes strong legal protections with full government support. It also takes a village, literally. A forest's most intimate neighbors must wholeheartedly want it saved, one generation after another. That theme repeats in places as different as rural Madagascar and suburban New Jersey.

1. _____

12 First a word about trees themselves. This *Science News* issue leans in with a magnifying glass to look at trees as a way to capture carbon and fight climate change. But trees are much more than useful wooden objects that happen to be leafy, self-manufacturing and great shade for picnics.

13 "Plant blindness," as it has been called, reduces trees and other photosynthetic organisms to background, lamented botanist Sandra Knapp in a 2019 article in the journal *Plants, People, Planet*. For instance, show people a picture with a squirrel in a forest. They'll likely say something like "cute squirrel". Not "nice-size beech tree, and is that a young black oak with a cute squirrel on it?

14 This tunnel vision also excludes invertebrates, argues Knapp, of the Natural History Museum in London, complicating efforts to save nature. These half-seen forests, natural plus human-planted, now cover close to a third of the planet's land, according to the 2020 version of "The State of the World's Forests" report from the United Nation's Food and Agriculture Organization. Yet a calculation based on the report's numbers says that over the last 10 years, net tree cover vanished at an average rate of about 12,990 hectares—a bit more than the area of San Francisco—every day (see Figure 8-1).

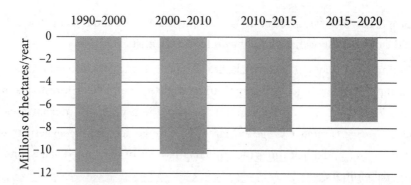

Figure 8-1　Annual Change in Area of Naturally Regenerating Forest, 1990–2020

15　This is an improvement over the previous decades, the report notes. In the 1990s, deforestation, on average, destroyed about 1.75 San Francisco equivalents of forest every day.

16　Trees were the planet's skyscrapers, many rising to great heights, hundreds of millions of years before humans began piling stone upon stone to build their own. Trees reach their stature by growing and then killing their innermost core of tissue. The still-living outer rim of the tree uses its ever-increasing inner ghost architecture as plumbing pipes that can function as long as several human lifetimes. And tree sex lives. Plants invented "steamy but not touchy" long before the Victorian novel-much flowering, perfuming and maybe green yearning, all without direct contact of reproductive organs. Just a dusting of pollen wafted on a breeze or delivered by a bee.

17　To achieve the all-important goal of cutting global emissions, saving the natural forests already in the ground must be a priority, 14 scientists from around the world wrote in the April *Global Change Biology*. "Protect existing forests first," coauthor Kate Hardwick of Kew Gardens in London said during a virtual conference on reforestation in February. That priority also gives the planet's magnificent biodiversity a better chance at surviving. Trees can store a lot of carbon in racing to the sky. And size and age matter because trees add carbon over so much of their architecture, says ecologist David Mildrexler with Eastern Oregon Legacy Lands at the Wallowology Natural History Discovery Center in Joseph. Trees don't just start new growth at twigs tipped with unfurling baby leaves. Inside the branches, the trunk and big roots, an actively growing sheath surrounds the inner ghost plumbing. Each season, this whole sheath adds a layer of carbon-capturing tissue from root to crown.

18　"Imagine you're standing in front of a really big tree—one that's so big you can't even wrap your arms all the way around, and you look up the trunk," Mildrexler says. Compare that sky-touching vision to the area covered in a year's growth of some sapling,

UNIT **8** Environment and Climate

maybe three fingers thick and human height. "The difference is, of course, just huge," he says.

19   Big trees may not be common, but they make an outsize difference in trapping carbon, Mildrexler and colleagues have found. In six Pacific Northwest national forests, only about 3 percent of all the trees in the study, including ponderosa pines, western larches and three other major species, reached full-arm-hug size (at least 53.3 centimeters in diameter). Yet this 3 percent of trees stored 42 percent of the above ground carbon there, the team reported in 2020 in *Frontiers in Forests and Global Change*. An earlier study, with 48 sites worldwide and more than 5 million tree trunks, found that the largest 1 percent of trees store about 50 percent of the above ground carbon-filled biomass.

2. _____

20   The island nation of Madagascar was an irresistible place for the Missouri Botanical Garden to start trying to conserve forests. Off the east coast of Africa, the island stretches more than the distance from Savannah, Ga., to Toronto, and holds more than 12,000 named species of trees, other flowering plants and ferns. Madagascar "is absolute nirvana", says MBG botanist James S. Miller, who has spent decades exploring the island's flora.

21   Just consider the rarities. Of the eight known species of baobab trees, which raise a fat trunk to a cartoonishly spindly tuft of little branches on top, six are native to Madagascar. Miller considers some 90 percent of the island's plants as natives unique to the country. "It wrecks you" for botanizing elsewhere, Miller says.

22   He was rooting for his MBG colleagues Randrianasolo and Birkinshaw in their foray to Madagascar's Agnalazaha forest. Several months after getting roasted as liars by residents, the two got word that the skeptics had decided to give protection a chance after all.

23   The Agnalazaha residents wanted to make sure, however, that the Missouri group realized the solemnity of their promise. Randrianasolo had to return to the island for a ceremony of calling the ancestors as witnesses to the new partnership and marking the occasion with the sacrifice of a cow. A pact with generations of deceased residents may be an unusual form of legal involvement, but it carried weight. Randrianasolo bought the cow.

24   Randrianasolo looked for ways to be helpful. MBG worked on improving the village's rice yields, and supplied starter batches of vegetable seeds for expanding home gardens. The MBG staff helped the forest residents apply for conservation funds from

the Malagasy government. A new tree nursery gave villagers an alternative to cutting timber in the forest. The nursery also meant some jobs for local people, which further improved relationships.

25   The MBG staff now works with Malagasy communities to preserve forests at 11 sites dotted in various ecosystems in Madagascar. Says Randrianasolo: "You have to be patient."

26   Today, 19 years after his first visit among the mourners, Agnalazaha still stands.

27   Saving forests is not a simple matter of just meeting basic needs of people living nearby, says political scientist Nadia Rabesahala Horning of Middlebury College in Vermont, who published *The Politics of Deforestation in Africa* in 2018. Her Ph.D. work, starting in the late 1990s, took her to four remote forests in her native Madagascar. The villagers around each forest followed different rules for harvesting timber, finding places to graze livestock and collecting medicinal plants.

28   Three of the forests shrank, two of them rapidly, over the decade. One, called Analavelona, however, barely showed any change in the aerial views Horning used to look for fraying forests.

29   The people living around Analavelona revered it as a sacred place where their ancestors dwelled. Living villagers made offerings before entering, and cut only one kind of tree, which they used for coffins.

30   Since then, Horning's research in Tanzania and Uganda has convinced her that forest conservation can happen only under very specific conditions, she says. The local community must be able to trust that the government won't let some commercial interest or a political heavy-weight slip through loopholes to exploit a forest that its everyday neighbors can't touch. And local people must be able to meet their own needs too, including the spiritual ones.

3. _____

31   Another constellation of old forests, on the other side of the world, sports some less-than-obvious similarities. Ecologist Joan Maloof launched the Old-Growth Forest Network in 2011 to encourage people to save the remaining scraps of U.S. old-growth forests. Her bold idea: to permanently protect one patch of old forest in each of the more than 2,000 counties in the United States where forests can grow.

32   She calls for strong legal measures, such as conservation easements that prevent logging, but also recognizes the need to convey the emotional power of communing with nature. One of the early green spots she and her colleagues campaigned for was

not old growth, but it had become one of the few left unlogged where she lived on Maryland's Eastern Shore.

33 She heard about Buddhist monks in Thailand who had ordained trees as monks because loggers revered the monks, so the trees were protected. A month after the 9/11 terrorist attacks, she was inspired to turn the Maryland forest into a place to remember the victims. By putting each victim's name on a metal tag and tying it to a tree, she and other volunteers created a memorial with close to 3,000 trees. The local planning commission, she suspected, would feel awkward about approving timber cutting from that particular stand. She wasn't party to their private deliberations, but the forest still stands.

34 As of Earth Day 2021, the network had about 125 forests around the country that should stay forests in perpetuity. Their stories vary widely, but are full of local history and political maneuvering.

35 In southern New Jersey, Joshua Saddler, an escaped enslaved man from Maryland, acquired part of a small forest in the mid-1880s and bequeathed it to his wife with the stipulation that it not be logged. His section was logged anyway, and the rest of the original old forest was about to meet the same fate. In 1973, high school student Doug Hefty wrote more than 80 pages on the forest's value—and delivered it to the developer. In this case, life delivered a genuine Hollywood ending. The developer relented, and scaled back the project, stopping across the street from the woods.

36 In 1999, however, developers once again eyed the forest, says Janet Goehner-Jacobs, who heads the Saddler's Woods Conservation Association. It took four years, but now, she and the forests' other fans have a conservation easement forbidding commercial development or logging, giving the next generation better tools to protect the forest.

37 Goehner-Jacobs had just moved to the area and fallen in love with that 10-hectare patch of green in the midst of apartment buildings and strip malls. When she first happened upon the forest and found the old-growth section, "I just instinctively knew I was seeing something very different." (*Science News*, July 3 & July 17, 2021)

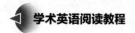

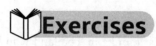

I Fast reading

Task 1 Tick (√) the statement that does not agree with the information in Paragraphs 1–11.

(   ) A. Botanist Randrianasolo is the first native of Madagascar to become a Ph.D.

(   ) B. The 2002 scouting trip, which Randrianasolo joined, is the first movement to carry out forest conservation in Madagascar.

(   ) C. The Missouri group planned to go small and focus on fragments of humid forest.

(   ) D. The two scientists of MBG showed up in an out-of-way village in Madagascar in bad timing.

Task 2 Tick (√) the statement that most closely reflects the writer's point of view.

(   ) A. The most important thing to fight climate change is to plant new trees.

(   ) B. Trees are emphasized and foregrounded in any case.

(   ) C. Saving today's forests ranks higher in priority in fighting climate change.

(   ) D. Success in protecting forests takes strong legal protections with a little government support.

Task 3 Match the headings with the numbered blanks within the text.

Heading	Number
A Different Kind of Essential	

UNIT **8** Environment and Climate

(Continued)

Heading	Number
Plant Paradise	
Overlooked and Underprotected	

II Annotating skills

Task 4 When you are reading an academic text, it is important to consider the function of sentences. Understanding how sentences work in unison helps you differentiate the main idea from the supporting ideas. Read the list below and complete the gap in each sentence with a word from the box.

link   secondary   idea   key   develop   write   explain

Sentences may:

- introduce a new _____ which is the focus of the paragraph.

- provide a _____ between paragraphs.

- _____ an idea which has already been introduced in the "focus" sentence.

- summarize the _____ point or points.

- introduce a _____ point.

Task 5 Complete the tables with the functions listed below. Find the details describing the function in the column of notes where * exists. Some sentences may have more than one function. The first one has been done for you.

- background information
- general problem
- solution
- exemplification
- cause
- explication
- implication
- evaluation
- viewpoint

179

- definition
- transition
- summary
- comparison & contrast
- conclusion

Paragraph 9

① Finding some way out of such clashes to save existing forests has become crucial for fighting climate change. ② Between 2001 and 2019, the planet's forests trapped an estimated 7.6 billion metric tons of carbon dioxide a year, an international team reported in *Nature Climate Change* in March. ③ That rough accounting suggests trees may capture about one and a half times the annual emissions of the United States, one of the largest global emitters.

Sentence	Function	Notes
①	viewpoint	
②		
③		

Paragraph 11

① How to preserve forests may be a harder question than why. ② Success takes strong legal protections with full government support. ③ It also takes a village, literally. ④ A forest's most intimate neighbors must wholeheartedly want it saved, one generation after another. ⑤ That theme repeats in places as different as rural Madagascar and suburban New Jersey.

Sentence	Function	Notes
①	transition	
②		
③		
④		*
⑤		

Paragraph 17

① To achieve the all-important goal of cutting global emissions, saving the natural forests already in the ground must be a priority, 14 scientists from around the world wrote in the April *Global Change Biology*. ② "Protect existing forests first," coauthor Kate Hardwick of Kew Gardens in London said during a virtual conference on reforestation in February. ③ That priority also gives the planet's magnificent biodiversity a better chance at surviving. ④ Trees can store a lot of carbon in racing to the sky. ⑤ And size and age matter because trees add carbon over so much of their architecture, says ecologist David Mildrexler with Eastern Oregon Legacy Lands at the Wallowology Natural History Discovery Center in Joseph. ⑥ Trees don't just start new growth at twigs tipped with unfurling baby leaves. ⑦ Inside the branches, the trunk and big roots, an actively growing sheath surrounds the inner ghost plumbing. ⑧ Each season, this whole sheath adds a layer of carbon-capturing tissue from root to crown.

Sentence	Function	Notes
①	viewpoint + cause	* saving today's forests must be a priority + cutting global emissions
②		*
③		*
④		*
⑤		*
⑥		*
⑦		*
⑧		*

III Reading for specific information

Task 6 Read Text A carefully, but as fast as you can. Try to answer as many questions as you can without referring to the text.

1. Who is the first native of Madagascar to become a Ph.D. taxonomist in MBG?

2. Who are the two scientists planning to protect the Agnalazaha forest?

3. Why did the Agnalazaha forest community refuse the two scientists' proposal of protection at the very beginning?

4. According to Sandra Knapp, what is the consequence of "plant blindness"?

5. Roughly, how big is the cover of natural plus human-planted trees? And averagely how much does net tree cover vanish every day?

6. How do trees reach their stature? And what does the still-living outer rim of the tree use as plumbing pipes?

7. Compared with sapling, how differently do big trees trap carbon?

8. Why does James S. Miller say Madagascar "is absolute nirvana"?

9. How long did Randrianasolo and Birkinshaw wait till they got word that the skeptics had decided to give protection a chance after getting roasted as liars by residents? On what condition did Agnalazaha residents give them a chance?

10. At how many protection sites do the MBG staff now work with Malagasy communities to preserve forests in Madagascar?

11. What has Horning's research in Tanzania and Uganda convinced her of?

12. Saving forests is not a simple matter of just meeting basic living needs of local people, but also the spiritual ones. Can you give an example?

13. What's the purpose of the Old-Growth Forest Network initiated by Maloof?

14. To what does Maloof resort to carry out her programme?

15. As of Earth Day 2021, how many forests did the network have around U.S. that should stay forests in perpetuity?

Task 7 Read the text and try to find the text-referring words in the table. Note down the idea or word(s) that each one refers to. The first one has been done for you.

Text-referring word(s)	Refers to...	Paragraph
The team zeroed in on fragments of humid forest	the Missouri group	4
The village was filling up with visiting relatives and acquaintances		6

UNIT 8 Environment and Climate

(Continued)

Text-referring word(s)	Refers to...	Paragraph
The community was still upset about a different forest		8
This tunnel vision also excludes invertebrates		14
This is an improvement over the previous decades		15
That priority also gives the planet's magnificent biodiversity a better chance at surviving		17
Just consider *the rarities*		21
He was rooting for his MBG colleagues Randrianasolo and Birkinshaw in their foray to Madagascar's Agnalazaha forest		22
the two got word that the skeptics had decided to give protection a chance after all		22
the network had about 125 forests around the country that should stay forests in perpetuity		34

IV Language enhancement

Task 8 Find the word in the text with the same or similar meaning to each of the expressions in the left column of the table below. The first one has been done for you.

Expression	Synonym in text	Paragraph
the protection of the natural environment	conservation	2
an animal like a monkey		3
to pull something hard		3
sadness that you show and feel because somebody has died		5
all the people who live in a particular area		5

183

(Continued)

Expression	Synonym in text	Paragraph
to admit that something is true, often unwillingly		6
having lost a relative or close friend who has recently died		6
the production or sending out of light, heat, gas		9
something that you think is more important than other things and should be dealt with first		10
remaining after all deductions		14
to stop existing		14
equal in value, amount, meaning, importance		15
larger than the usual size		19
(in the religion of Buddhism) the state of peace and happiness that a person achieves after giving up all personal desires		20
trees that are grown to be used in building or for making things		24
in or belonging to the air		28
to feel great respect or admiration for somebody/something		29
to live somewhere		29
something offered, especially to God		29
a small mistake in the law which allows people to do something that would otherwise be illegal		30
to treat a person or situation as an opportunity to gain an advantage for yourself		30
to describe situations that seem to exist all the time		31
to make somebody a priest, minister or rabbi		33
to act in order to achieve a certain goal		34
to finally agree to something after refusing		35

UNIT **8** Environment and Climate

Task 9 Study the words or phrases in the table below and identify them in the text. Try to work out their meanings by using the context in which you find them without using a dictionary. The first one has been done for you.

Word or phrase	Possible meaning	Paragraph
reception	the way a person or a group of people react to someone or something	7
pitch		7
lumber		8
off-limits		8
poacher		8
clash		9
tunnel vision		14
stature		16
twig		17
sheath		17
sapling		18
rarity		21
root for		22
roast		22
carry weight		23
shrink		28
ancestor		29
sport		31
log		32
call for		32
bequeath		35
scale back		35

Task 10 Locate the phrases in the text and complete the table below by explaining, in your own words, the meaning of each italicized word. Pay attention to the writer's choice of the adjective or adverb for emphasis. The first one has been done for you.

Phrase	Meaning	Paragraph
hardly the best time	to modify a statement when you want to emphasize that it is only a small amount which makes it true, and that therefore it is best to consider the opposite statement as being true	1
preferably forests with lots of …		3
still be able to		8
wholeheartedly want it		11
all-important goal		17
can't *even* wrap your arms		18
outsize difference		19
barely showed		28
very *specific* conditions		30
widely vary		34

V Reading skills: Examining graphics

Task 11 Academic texts often include expressions about changes over a period of time. Some common ways of describing changes over time are shown in the tables below. You can add as many as you can.

	Adverb	Adjective
Has become / became	less	common
	_____	_____
	_____	_____

UNIT **8** Environment and Climate

(Continued)

	Adverb	Adjective
	_____	_____
	_____	
	_____	
	_____	
	_____	

	Adjective	Noun
	slight	increase
There has been / there was a	_____	_____
	_____	_____
	_____	_____
	_____	_____

Task 12 Read Figure 8-1 in Text A. Work with a partner and answer the questions below in your own words.

1. What does the figure show?

2. What do the points along the invisible *y* axis (the vertical line) represent?

3. What is the forest loss in the decade from 1990 through 2000?

4. What is the forest loss in the decade from 2010 through 2020?

5. Can you describe the change between the two different time periods in the last two questions?

187

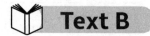

The Promise and Pitfalls of Trees

Carolyn Gramling

1. Trees are symbols of hope, life and transformation. They're also increasingly touted as a straightforward, relatively inexpensive, ready-for-prime-time solution to climate change.

2. When it comes to removing human-caused emissions of the greenhouse gas carbon dioxide from Earth's atmosphere, trees are a big help. Through photosynthesis, trees pull the gas out of the air to help grow their leaves, branches and roots. Forest soils can also sequester vast reservoirs of carbon.

3. Earth holds, by one estimate, as many as 3 trillion trees. Enthusiasm is growing among governments, businesses and individuals for ambitious projects to plant billions, even a trillion more. Such massive tree-planting projects, advocates say, could do two important things: help offset current emissions and also draw out CO_2 emissions that have lingered in the atmosphere for decades or longer.

4. Even in the politically divided United States, large-scale tree-planting projects have broad bipartisan support, according to a spring 2020 poll by the Pew Research Center. And over the last decade, a diverse garden of tree-centric proposals—from planting new seedlings to promoting natural regrowth of degraded forests to blending trees with crops and pasturelands—has sprouted across the international political landscape.

5. Trees "are having a bit of a moment right now," says Joe Fargione, an ecologist with The Nature Conservancy who is based in Minneapolis. It helps that everybody likes trees. "There's no anti-tree lobby. [Trees] have lots of benefits for people. Not only do they store carbon, they help provide clean air, prevent soil erosion, shade and shelter homes to reduce energy costs and give people a sense of well-being."

6. Conservationists are understandably eager to harness this enthusiasm to combat climate change. "We're tapping into the zeitgeist," says Justin Adams, executive director of the Tropical Forest Alliance at the World Economic Forum, an international nongovernmental organization based in Geneva. In January 2020, the World Economic Forum launched the One Trillion Trees Initiative, a global movement to grow, restore and conserve trees around the planet. One trillion is also the target for other organizations that coordinate global forestation projects, such

as Plant-for-the-Planet's Trillion Tree Campaign and Trillion Trees, a partnership of the World Wildlife Fund, the Wildlife Conservation Society and other conservation groups.

7   Yet, as global eagerness for adding more trees grows, some scientists are urging caution. Before moving forward, they say, such massive tree projects must address a range of scientific, political, social and economic concerns. Poorly designed projects that don't address these issues could do more harm than good, the researchers say, wasting money as well as political and public goodwill. The concerns are myriad: There's too much focus on numbers of seedlings planted, and too little time spent on how to keep the trees alive in the long term, or in working with local communities. And there's not enough emphasis on how different types of forests sequester very different amounts of carbon. There's too much talk about trees, and not enough about other carbon-storing ecosystems.

8   "There's a real feeling that… forests and trees are just the idea we can use to get political support" for many, perhaps more complicated, types of landscape restoration initiatives, says Joseph Veldman, an ecologist at Texas A&M University in College Station. But that can lead to all kinds of problems, he adds. "For me, the devil is in the details."

1. _____

9   The pace of climate change is accelerating into the realm of emergency, scientists say. Over the last 200 years, human-caused emissions of greenhouse gases, including CO_2 and methane, have raised the average temperature of the planet by about 1 degree Celsius.

10   The litany of impacts of this heating is familiar by now. Earth's poles are rapidly shedding ice, which raises sea levels; the oceans are heating up, threatening fish and food security. Tropical storms are becoming rainier and lingering longer, and out of control wildfires are blazing from the Arctic to Australia.

11   The world's oceans and land-based ecosystems, such as forests, absorb about half of the carbon emissions from fossil fuel burning and other industrial activities. The rest goes into the atmosphere. So "the majority of the solutions to climate change will need to come from reducing our emissions," Fargione says. To meet climate targets set by the 2015 Paris Agreement, much deeper and more painful cuts in emissions than nations have pledged so far will be needed in the next 10 years.

12   But increasingly, scientists warn that reducing emissions alone won't be enough

to bring Earth's thermostat back down. "We really do need an all-hands-on-deck approach," Fargione says. Specifically, researchers are investigating ways to actively remove that carbon, known as negative emissions technologies. Many of these approaches, such as removing CO_2 directly from the air and converting it into fuel, are still being developed.

13 But trees are a ready kind of negative emissions technology, and many researchers see them as the first line of defense. In its January 2020 report, "Carbon Shot," the World Resources Institute, a global nonprofit research organization, suggested that large and immediate investments in reforestation within the United States will be key for the country to have any hope of reaching carbon neutrality—in which ongoing carbon emissions are balanced by carbon withdrawals—by 2050. The report called for the U.S. government to invest $4 billion a year through 2030 to support tree restoration projects across the United States. Those efforts would be a bridge to a future of, hopefully, more technologies that can pull large amounts of carbon out of the atmosphere.

2. _____

14 Earth's forests absorb, on average, 16 billion metric tons of CO_2 annually, researchers reported in the March *Nature Climate Change*. But human activity can turn forests into sources of carbon: Thanks to land clearing, wildfires and the burning of wood products, forests also emit an estimated 8.1 billion tons of the gas back to the atmosphere.

15 That leaves a net amount of 7.6 billion tons of CO_2 absorbed by forests per year—roughly a fifth of the 36 billion tons of CO_2 emitted by humans in 2019. Deforestation and forest degradation are rapidly shifting the balance. Forests in Southeast Asia now emit more carbon than they absorb due to clearing for plantations and uncontrolled fires. The Amazon's forests may flip from carbon sponge to carbon source by 2050, researchers say. The priority for slowing climate change, many agree, should be saving the trees we have.

16 Just how many more trees might be mustered for the fight is unclear, however. In 2019, Thomas Crowther, an ecologist at ETH Zurich, and his team estimated in *Science* that around the globe, there are 900 million hectares of land—an area about the size of the United States—available for planting new forests and reviving old ones. That land could hold over a trillion more trees, the team claimed, which could trap about 206 billion tons of carbon over a century.

17 That study, led by Jean-Francois Bastin, then a postdoc in Crowther's lab, was

sweeping, ambitious and hopeful. Its findings spread like wildfire through media, conservationist and political circles. "We were in New York during Climate Week [2019], and everybody's talking about this paper," Adams recalls. "It had just popped into people's consciousness, this unbelievable technology solution called the tree."

18   To channel that enthusiasm, the One Trillion Trees Initiative incorporated the study's findings into its mission statement, and countless other tree-planting efforts have cited the report.

19   But critics say the study is deeply flawed, and that its accounting—of potential trees, of potential carbon uptake—is not only sloppy, but dangerous. In 2019, *Science* published five separate responses outlining numerous concerns. For example, the study's criteria for "available" land for tree planting were too broad, and the carbon accounting was inaccurate because it assumes that new tree canopy cover equals new carbon storage. Savannas and natural grasslands may have relatively few trees, critics noted, but these regions already hold plenty of carbon in their soils. When that carbon is accounted for, the carbon uptake benefit from planting trees drops to perhaps a fifth of the original estimate.

20   There's also the question of how forests themselves can affect the climate. Adding trees to snow-covered regions, for example, could increase the absorption of solar radiation, possibly leading to warming.

21   "Their numbers are just so far from anything reasonable," Veldman says. And focusing on the number of trees planted also sets up another problem, he adds—an incentive structure that is prone to corruption. "Once you set up the incentive system, behaviors change to basically play that game."

22   Adams acknowledges these concerns. But, the One Trillion Trees Initiative isn't really focused on "the specifics of the math", he says, whether it's the number of trees or the exact amount of carbon sequestered. The goal is to create a powerful climate movement to "motivate a community behind a big goal and a big vision", he says. "It could give us a fighting chance to get restoration right."

23   Other nonprofit conservation groups, like the World Resources Institute and The Nature Conservancy, are trying to walk a similar line in their advocacy. But some scientists are skeptical that governments and policy makers tasked with implementing massive forest restoration programs will take note of such nuances.

24   "I study how government bureaucracy works," says Forrest Fleischman, who researches forest and environmental policy at the University of Minnesota in St. Paul. Policy makers, he says, are "going to see 'forest restoration', and that means planting

rows of trees. That's what they know how to do."

3. _____

25 How much carbon a forest can draw from the atmosphere depends on how you define "forest". There is reforestation—restoring trees to regions where they used to be—and afforestation—planting new trees where they haven't historically been. Reforestation can mean new planting, including crop trees; allowing forests to regrow naturally on lands previously cleared for agriculture or other purposes; or blending tree cover with croplands or grazing areas.

26 In the past, the carbon uptake potential of letting forests regrow naturally was underestimated by 32 percent, on average—and by as much as 53 percent in tropical forests, according to a 2020 study in *Nature*. Now, scientists are calling for more attention to this forestation strategy.

27 If it's just a matter of what's best for the climate, natural forest regrowth offers the biggest bang for the buck, says Simon Lewis, a forest ecologist at University College London. Single-tree commercial crop plantations, on the other hand, may meet the technical definition of a "forest"—a certain concentration of trees in a given area—but factor in land clearing to plant the crop and frequent harvesting of the trees, and such plantations can actually release more carbon than they sequester.

28 Comparing the carbon accounting between different restoration projects becomes particularly important in the framework of international climate targets and challenges. For example, the 2011 Bonn Challenge is a global project aimed at restoring 350 million hectares by 2030. As of 2020, 61 nations had pledged to restore a total of 210 million hectares of their lands. The potential carbon impact of the stated pledges, however, varies widely depending on the specific restoration plans.

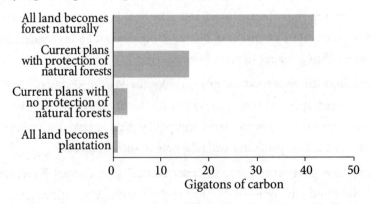

Figure 8-2 Amount of Carbon Sequestered by 2100 in Four Bonn Challenge Scenarios

29 In a 2019 study in *Nature*, Lewis and his colleagues estimated that if all 350 million hectares were allowed to regrow natural forest, those lands would sequester about 42 billion metric tons (gigatons in Figure 8-2) of carbon by 2100. Conversely, if the land were to be filled with single-tree commercial crop plantations, carbon storage drops to about 1 billion metric tons. And right now, plantations make up a majority of the restoration plans submitted under the Bonn Challenge.

30 Striking the right balance between offering incentives to landowners to participate while also placing certain restrictions remains a tricky and long-standing challenge, not just for combating the climate emergency but also for trying to preserve biodiversity. Since 1974, Chile, for example, has been encouraging private landowners to plant trees through subsidies. But landowners are allowed to use these subsidies to replace native forestlands with profitable plantations. As a result, Chile's new plantings not only didn't increase carbon storage, they also accelerated biodiversity losses, researchers reported in the September 2020 *Nature Sustainability*.

31 The reality is that plantations are a necessary part of initiatives like the Bonn Challenge, because they make landscape restoration economically viable for many nations, Lewis says. "Plantations can play a part, and so can agroforestry as well as areas of more natural forest," he says. "It's important to remember that landscapes provide a whole host of services and products to people who live there."

32 But he and others advocate for increasing the proportion of forestation that is naturally regenerated. "I'd like to see more attention on that," says Robin Chazdon, a forest ecologist affiliated with the University of the Sunshine Coast in Australia as well as with the World Resources Institute. Naturally regenerated forests could be allowed to grow in buffer regions between farms, creating connecting green corridors that could also help preserve biodiversity, she says. And "it's certainly a lot less expensive to let nature do the work," Chazdon says.

33 Indeed, massive tree-planting projects may also be stymied by pipeline and workforce issues. Take seeds: In the United States, nurseries produce about 1.3 billion seedlings per year, Fargione and colleagues calculated in a study reported February 4 in *Frontiers in Forests and Global Change*. To support a massive tree-planting initiative, U.S. nurseries would need to at least double that number.

4. _____

34 Countries around the world have launched enthusiastic national tree-planting efforts. And many of them have become cautionary tales.

35   Recently, Turkey launched its own reforestation effort. On November 11, 2019, National Forestation Day, volunteers across the country planted 11 million trees at more than 2,000 sites. In Turkey's Çorum Province, 303,150 saplings were planted in a single hour, setting a new world record.

36   Within three months, however, up to 90 percent of the new saplings inspected by Turkey's agriculture and forestry trade union were dead, according to the union's president, Şükrü Durmuş, speaking to the *Guardian* (Turkey's minister of agriculture and forestry denied that this was true). The saplings, Durmuş said, died due to a combination of insufficient water and because they were planted at the wrong time of year, and not by experts.

37   Some smaller-scale efforts also appear to be failing, though less spectacularly. Tree planting has been ongoing for decades in the Kangra district of Himachal Pradesh in northern India, says Eric Coleman, a political scientist at Florida State University in Tallahassee, who's been studying the outcomes. The aim is to increase the density of the local forests and provide additional forest benefits for communities nearby, such as wood for fuel and fodder for grazing animals. How much money was spent isn't known, Coleman says, because there aren't records of how much was paid for seeds. "But I imagine it was in the millions and millions of dollars."

38   Coleman and his colleagues analyzed satellite images and interviewed members of the local communities. They found that the tree planting had very little impact one way or the other. Forest density didn't change much, and the surveys suggested that few households were gaining benefits from the planted forests, such as gathering wood for fuel, grazing animals or collecting fodder.

39   But massive tree-planting efforts don't have to fail. It's easy to point to examples of large-scale reforestation efforts that weren't using the right tree stock, or adequately trained workforces, or didn't have enough investment in... postplanting treatments and care, "Fargione says. "We need to learn from those efforts."

5. _____

40   Forest Lalisa Duguma of World Agroforestry in Nairobi, Kenya, and his colleagues explored some of the reasons for the very high failure rates of these projects in a working paper in 2020. "Every year there are billions of dollars invested [in tree planting], but forest cover is not increasing," Duguma says. "Where are those reasons going?"

41   In 2019, Duguma raised this question at the World Congress on Agroforestry in Montpellier, France. He asked the audience of scientists and conservationists: "How

many of you have ever planted a tree seedling?" To those who raised their hands, he asked, "Have they grown?"

42   Some respondents acknowledged that they weren't sure. "Very good! That's what I wanted," he told them. "We invest a lot in tree plantings, but we are not sure what happens after that."

43   It comes down to a deceptively simple but "really fundamental" point, Duguma says. "The narrative has to change-from tree planting to tree growing."

44   The good news is that this point has begun to percolate through the conservationist world, he says. To have any hope of success, restoration projects need to consider the best times of year to plant seeds, which seeds to plant and where, who will care for the seedlings as they grow into trees, how that growth will be monitored, and how to balance the economic and environmental needs of people in developing countries where the trees might be planted.

45   "That is where we need to capture the voice of the people," Duguma says. "From the beginning."

46   Even as the enthusiasm for tree planting takes root in the policy world, there's a growing awareness among researchers and conservationists that local community engagement must be built into these plans; it's indispensable to their success.

47   It will be almost impossible to meet these targets we all care so much about unless small farmers and communities benefit more from trees," as David Kaimowitz of the United Nations' Food and Agriculture Organization wrote March 19 in a blog post for the London-based nonprofit International Institute for Environment and Development.

48   For one thing, farmers and villagers managing the land need incentives to care for the plantings and that includes having clear rights to the trees' benefits, such as food or thatching or grazing. "People who have insecure land tenure don't plant trees," Fleischman says.

49   Fleischman and others outlined many of the potential social and economic pitfalls of large-scale tree-planting projects last November in *BioScience*. Those lessons boil down to this, Fleischman says: "You need to know something about the place... the political dynamics, the social dynamics... It's going to be very different in different parts of the world."

50   The old cliché—think globally, act locally—may offer the best path forward for conservationists and researchers trying to balance so many different needs and still address climate change.

51 "There are a host of sociologically and biologically informed approaches to conservation and restoration that... have virtually nothing to do with tree planting," Veldman says. "An effective global restoration agenda needs to encompass the diversity of Earth's ecosystems and the people who use them." (*Science News*, July 3 & July 17, 2021)

Exercises

I Fast reading

Task 1 Tick (√) the statement that most closely reflects the writer's point of view.

(　) A. Reducing emissions alone is enough to bring Earth's thermostat back down.

(　) B. Planting trees is the only way to eradicate the risk of global warming.

(　) C. The best way to combat climate change is planting trees.

(　) D. Massive planting projects need much more planning and follow-through to counter climate change.

Task 2 Match the headings with the numbered blanks within the text.

Heading	Number
The Numbers Game	
A Tree-planting Report Card	
The Root of the Problem	
Speak for the Trees	
Counting Carbon	

UNIT 8 Environment and Climate

II Annotating skills

Task 3 Complete the table with the functions listed below. Find the details describing the function in the column of notes where * exists. Some sentences may have more than one function. The first one has been done for you.

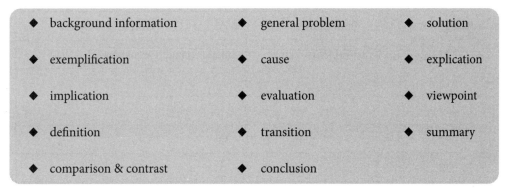

- background information
- general problem
- solution
- exemplification
- cause
- explication
- implication
- evaluation
- viewpoint
- definition
- transition
- summary
- comparison & contrast
- conclusion

① Yet, as global eagerness for adding more trees grows, some scientists are urging caution. ② Before moving forward, they say, such massive tree projects must address a range of scientific, political, social and economic concerns. ③ Poorly designed projects that don't address these issues could do more harm than good, the researchers say, wasting money as well as political and public goodwill. ④ The concerns are myriad: There's too much focus on numbers of seedlings planted, and too little time spent on how to keep the trees alive in the long term, or in working with local communities. ⑤ And there's not enough emphasis on how different types of forests sequester very different amounts of carbon. ⑥ There's too much talk about trees, and not enough about other carbon-storing ecosystems.

Sentence	Function	Notes
①	transition	* linking the previous information and introducing the following
②		*
③		
④		
⑤		*
⑥		

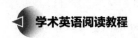

Task 4 Complete the table with the functions listed in Task 3. Find the details describing the function in the column of notes where * exists. Some paragraphs may have more than one function. The first one has been done for you.

Section: The Root of the Problem

Paragraph	Function	Notes
9	general problem + cause	* climate change + emissions
10		*
11		*
12		
13		*

Section: A Tree-planting Report Card

Paragraph(s)	Function	Notes
34	viewpoint	* Tree-planting efforts in many countries have become cautionary tales.
35–36		*
37–38		*
39		

III Reading for specific information

Task 5 Read Text B carefully, but as fast as you can. Try to answer as many questions as you can without referring to the texts.

1. How can trees pull the gas out of the air to help grow their leaves, branches and roots?

2. Can forest soils sequester vast reservoirs of carbon?

3. What are the two important things massive tree-planting projects could do?

UNIT 8 Environment and Climate

4. What is the root of climate change?

5. According to Joe Fargione, what is the majority of the solutions to climate change?

6. What is a ready kind of negative emissions technology?

7. How do you define carbon neutrality?

8. Due to what factors do forests emit the estimated 8.1 billion tons of the gas back to the atmosphere?

9. What is the rough proportion of CO_2 absorbed by forests in the total CO_2 emitted by humans in 2019?

10. What is the priority for slowing climate change?

11. Why do critics say that the study led by Jean-Francois Bastin, then a postdoc in Crowther's lab, is deeply flawed? Can you give at least one reason?

12. What do reforestation and afforestation mean respectively?

13. Which is better for the climate, reforestation or afforestation?

14. How can we improve the chances of success in massive tree-planting efforts?

15. What does an effective global restoration agenda need to encompass?

Task 6 Read the text and try to find the text-referring words in the table. Note down the idea or word(s) that each one refers to.

Text-referring word(s)	Refers to...	Paragraph
Conservationists are understandably eager to harness *this enthusiasm* to combat climate change	to plant billions, even a trillion more trees	6
But *that* can lead to all kinds of problems		8
But critics say *the study* is deeply flawed		19
But *he* and others advocate for increasing the proportion of forestation		32

(Continued)

Text-referring word(s)	Refers to...	Paragraph
The good news is that *this point* has begun to percolate through the conservationist world		44
and *that* includes having clear rights to the trees' benefits		48

IV Language enhancement

Task 7 Find the word in the text with the same or similar meaning to each of the expressions in the left column of the table below. The first one has been done for you.

Expression	Synonym in text	Paragraph
to try to persuade people that somebody/something is important or valuable by praising it	tout	1
to set apart from something else		2
an inquiry into public opinion conducted by interviewing a random sample of people		4
to use the power of		6
the spirit of the time		6
to bring into common action, movement, or condition		6
to happen faster		9
a long boring account of a series of events, reasons, etc.		10
to gather together		16
something that encourages you to do something		21
a very slight difference in meaning, sound, color or somebody's feeling		23
money paid by a government to an enterprise that benefits the public		30
having or showing a lot of knowledge about a particular subject or situation		51

UNIT **8** Environment and Climate

Task 8 Study the words or phrases in the table below and identify them in the text. Try to work out their meanings by using the context in which you find them without using a dictionary. The first one has been done for you.

Word or phrase	Possible meaning	Paragraph
massive	extremely large	3
soil erosion		5
tap		6
address		7
sweeping		17
pop (into)		17
flaw		19
uptake		19
the biggest bang for the buck		27
stymie		33
boil down		49

Task 9 Locate the phrase in the text and complete the table below by explaining the meaning of each italicized word in your own words. Pay attention to the writer's choice of the adjective or adverb for emphasis. The first one has been done for you.

Phrase	Meaning	Paragraph
increasingly touted	to indicate that a situation or quality is becoming greater in intensity or more common	1
are *understandably* eager to		6
deeply flawed		19
relatively few		19
anything *reasonable*		21

201

(Continued)

Phrase	Meaning	Paragraph
a *powerful* climate movement		22
cautionary tales		34
deceptively simple		43
think *globally*		50
act *locally*		50

V Reading skills: Examining graphics

Task 10 Study the language in the following tables carefully and find examples of language patterns both in Text A and Text B.

Verb	Adverb or adverb phrase
(has) increased	considerably
(has) decreased	significantly
has gone up (or down) / went up (or down)	somewhat
has fallen	a little
has dropped (to)	(by) XX percent
has shrank	rapidly
has vanished	drastically
has grown	gradually

Adverb	Quantity verb
(has) almost	doubled
(has) more than	tripled

Examples:

1. _____

_____

UNIT **8** Environment and Climate

2. _____

_____

Task 11 Use the above-mentioned language patterns to describe Figure 8-2 in Text B with at least two sentences.

_____

_____